CITY OF WIDOWS

CITY OF WIDOWS

An Iraqi Woman's Account of War and Resistance

Haifa Zangana

SEVEN STORIES PRESS

new york london melbourne toronto

Seven Stories Press
140 Watts Street
New York, NY 10013
www.sevenstories.com

In Canada: Publishers Group Canada, 559 College Street, Suite 402, Toronto, ON
M6G 1A9

In the UK: Turnaround Publisher Services Ltd., Unit 3, Olympia Trading Estate,
Coburg Road, Wood Green, London N22 6TZ

In Australia: Palgrave Macmillan, 15–19 Claremont Street, South Yarra VIC 3141

College professors may order examination copies of Seven Stories Press titles for a free
six-month trial period. To order, visit http://www.sevenstories.com/textbook or send a
fax on school letterhead to (212) 226-1411.

Book design by Hello {NYC}

Library of Congress Cataloging-in-Publication Data
Zangana, Haifa, 1950-
   City of widows : an Iraqi woman's account of war and resistance / Haifa Zangana. --
Seven Stories Press 1st ed.
      p. cm.
   ISBN 978-1-58322-779-4 (hardcover)
   ISBN 978-1-58322-860-9 (paperback)
   1. Zangana, Haifa, 1950- 2. Iraq War, 2003---Personal narratives, Iraqi. 3. Women--
Iraq--Biography. I. Title.
DS79.76.Z357 2008
956.7044´30922--dc22

                                    2007034335
Printed in the USA.

9 8 7 6 5 4 3 2 1

To the memory of A'beer Qassim Hamza al-Janaby, the fourteen-year-old girl who was gang-raped and set on fire by US troops in Mahmudiyah, twenty miles south of Baghdad, on March 12, 2006.

Contents

Preface
to the Paperback Edition

At the beginning of 2009, Iraq remains the scene of continuous mass destruction. Since the 2003 invasion, now whitewashed by the fiction of reduced violence, Iraqi women have continued to shoulder the brunt of daily tragedy with more fragmented households and more orphans.

The occupation continues to bring Iraqis nothing but massive loss of life, the destruction of homes and basic services, and diminishing faith in democracy. It also has not spared the occupiers. The ongoing economic crisis of the US and the global economies must be factored into the direct costs of over $12 billion a month for the last five years, with no clear end in sight. Some US economists, such as Joseph Stiglitz, estimate the total cost of the war to be over $3 trillion, when counting care for the long-term injured. The US-led occupation of Iraq has also brought instability to the whole region, the growth of the "axis of evil" it was purported to fight, and the spread of chaos to allies like Pakistan and Turkey, among others. Americans do not feel safer than they did before the 2003 invasion.

In the last two years, there has been a change in US tactics in dealing with Iraqis, men and women alike. Here is a look, by no means inclusive, of these changes, and of how they have been presented to the public.

SECURITY

Claims of "improved security" in Iraq in the last two years only mean fewer US casualties, covering up what General David Petraeus calls "sustainable violence" and sectarian and ethnic cleansing.

To reduce US casualties following the US troop surge in 2007, more Iraqis have been collectively punished, Israeli-style. The list of our dead from air strikes is long. According to a military statement, in what is counted as a single US air strike in January 2008, planes dropped 40,000 pounds of explosives during a ten-minute blitz on forty targets in the Jbour neighborhood in southern Baghdad. Targets are mostly civilian, including the homes of women and children, which the military invariably claim as terrorist sanctuaries. In 2007, the US military conducted more than five times as many air strikes in Iraq as it did in 2006, resulting in the murder of many more women and children.

On the ground, the anxious US military often kills Iraqi citizens going about their business, then plants evidence to cover up their mistakes, supposedly getting rid of "suspected al-Qaeda members." Facing mounting resistance across the country, the US military found the earlier labels of Sunni and Shi'ite invalid, and thus rebranded the resistance as al-Qaeda. It has become common for the US military to claim it has been battling Iranian-backed al-Qaeda as well as Iranian "special groups," a convenient buildup to a possible US attack on Iran.

For Iraqis themselves, who are either forgotten by the US and British governments or seen as terrorists' facilitators, the "security gains" since 2003 have not translated into fewer pre-dawn house raids, arbitrary arrests, kidnappings, car bombs in crowded markets, or killings by mercenaries called security employees who enjoy immunity from Iraqi and US courts of law. In October 2008, for example, daily atrocities continued to occur in Baghdad, Ninevah, Saladin, Najaf, and Anbar. This is no different from 2007, or 2006. Fear of death, planned or accidental, permeates the society to the degree of paralyzing it, or forcing people to live in a trance. What you see in the resilience of Iraqis continuing despite all is not due to gains in security, but to an overwhelming desperation to scrub a living and care for one's own.

In Baghdad and Mosul in the northern Nineveh province, security has declined amid a rise in car bombings and attacks directed mainly at government troops. Snipers have returned to the city but now aim their bullets solely at Iraqi troops.[1]

The crisis in Mosul, the third largest city in Iraq, is becoming increasingly desperate. Several thousand Arab Christians have fled their homes and taken refuge in churches in the city and on nearby mountains. The United Nations Refugee Agency (UNHCR) reported that about 13,000 people had been forced from their homes in October—more than half of the city's Christian community.[2] Some claim that Kurdish militias are trying to empty the city of Arab Christians before the upcoming local elections. Some claim that regional forces, including Israeli Mossad agents, bent on the clash of religions and cultures, are active among the militias.

Other cities are on the edge of disaster. The multiethnic, oil-rich city of Kirkuk, 250 kilometers northeast of Baghdad, sits on a volcano of political tension. Violent conflict could erupt if decisions on the future of the city are imposed according to sectarian and ethnic political loyalties rather than to the country as one.

THE SURGE

The highly publicized "success of the surge"—the US soldier increase of 30,000—in Baghdad was preceded by major population shifts based on sectarian cleansing. Previously mixed neighborhoods of Baghdad, where citizens cohabited regardless of religion or sect, became homogenized Sunni or Shi'ite Muslim enclaves.[3] Thus the road was paved for occupation forces to draw the new map of sectarian-divided Baghdad.

Post-surge Baghdad is no longer the magnificent capital of Iraq but a hideously scarred city with barriers, checkpoints, and walls. Every wall hems in a small neighborhood, leaving one entry checkpoint and one exit, dividing closely linked communities into smaller ghettos and gated communities. These walls are called "security walls" in official statements and inside the Green Zone, while the Iraqis call them "occupation walls" and make comparisons to the Israeli-built apartheid wall dividing Palestinians along the length of the West Bank.

Building segregation walls and destroying bridges means that hardly any mixed religious, ethnic areas can exist, enforcing the policy of divide and conquer, with many of the mixed-marriage families forced either to flee or hide themselves, often paying thugs for protection.

Walls, especially in Baghdad, are made of three-meter-high concrete blocks. During the surge, "the coalition forces [had] erected more than 3,000 individual sections of concrete blast walls throughout the city. . . . [These] barriers included both Jersey barriers—short concrete dividers commonly seen on roadways in the United States—and larger 20-foot blast walls that commonly surround bases and living areas."[4]

Before the surge in Baghdad and the erection of these concrete block walls, the US military isolated towns and villages with earthen walls and trenches. Several western towns on the Euphrates River were walled, from the legendary Fallujah, about thirty-five kilometers west of Baghdad, to Al Qaim near the Syrian border, 300 kilometers further west. In Haditha, where the massacre known as Iraq's My Lai took place, a sand wall twenty kilometers high sealed off the city of 80,000 inhabitants. A huge sand barrier was constructed around Tal Afar, near the Syrian border in the far north of the country. The first city to be walled in the Tigris basin was the shrine city of Samarra,[5] fifty kilometers north of Baghdad, and then Beiji, halfway to Mosel.

In these walled-in towns and cities, US forces and Iraqi police control the entry and exit roads at checkpoints using metal wand detectors and explosive-detection dogs. Residents must carry ID badges with an iris scan and fingerprints, and they need permission to travel outside the walls of their own town or city.[6] A process called the Biometric screening is being developed.[7]

There are fourteen totally enclosed areas in Baghdad now. Former sprawling and intermingling communities have been split into gated communities, potentially controllable by remote surveillance, rapid response military units, and air power.

RECONSTRUCTION AND SERVICES

In the six years of occupation, despite highly allocated funds being spent in Iraq, no strategic infrastructure has been repaired in the country. The failure of the US administration to repair the national electrical grid is especially remarkable because American contractors and Iraqi subcontractors depend on it to pump water and sewage. A recent report by the International Committee of the Red Cross (ICRC) indicates that "far too many Iraqis still have no choice but to drink dirty water and live in insalubrious conditions; this leads to more sick people seeking treatment in a healthcare system already stretched to the limit. But where do people get clean water? Furthermore, many Iraqis have to live with the health hazards of uncollected household waste and untreated sewage. As a result, many people contract water-borne diseases, further straining hospitals and clinics already struggling with a lack of resources."[8] By October 2008, cholera has spread in six of the eighteen provinces, with official figures of 771 cases, including nine fatalities.[9]

While there has been virtually no indigenous production in Iraq since 2005, federal budgets indicate that the number of government employees has nearly doubled from 1.2 million to 2.3 million.[10] Iraqis are paid to not work. "Corruption levels can mean the difference between life and death, when money for hospitals or clean water is in play," said Huguette Labelle, chair of Transparency International.[11] Billions of dollars from the public budget are spent on what is called security for officials, a euphemism for providing largesse to the new elite.

Students are encouraged to stay within their own walled-in districts through the offer of special courses to avoid traveling. Classes and exams are nominal; phony attendance figures create a façade of continuity. Neighborhoods are encouraged to be self-sufficient, instead of organically linked to one another. Unscrupulous traders, in connivance with security officials, are profiting recklessly by controlling the flow of goods in and out of restricted districts. The collapse of large hospitals means that the public relies on local care, mostly private and beyond the reach of most citizens.

REFUGEES AND RECONCILIATION

Though the invasion of Iraq has caused the consolidation of scores of local and national militias, the US continues to claim that Iraqis are fighting one another, and that the US's role has been to reconcile them. Their preferred solution has been to move populations around and/or to depopulate areas that are difficult for the US to control—that is, that have no pliable militias to use in service of American goals.

Recently, the US has officially funded the militias of the tribal Sunni councils called *al-Sahwa* (the awakening). These groups include members who have fought US troops, but are also said to loath al-Qaeda. The US has somewhat accommodated local resistance groups, bypassing the head of the US-sponsored government in the Green Zone in Baghdad. By mid-2008, there were over 300 such armed local groups with renewable short-term contracts funded by the US military, under the guise of integrating them into the Iraqi government security forces. Meanwhile, the official security forces are mainly comprised of members of other militias, and the Baghdad government sees the new groups as a potential threat. Al-Sahwa councils have succeeded momentarily to ease the pain of US forces, but they are clearly not a stable ally to either the US or the new Iraqi government. The future prospects for al-Sahwa members are growing dim as their rival sectarian militias in the government perpetuate murderous campaigns, and as Maliki's government refuses to employ all of them in the army and security forces as they were promised by the US. Iraqi security forces have arrested multiple al-Sahwa leaders and disbanded some of the troops. The uncertainty of their future could lead to civil war.

REFUGEES AND THE DISPLACED

The UNHCR estimates that more than 4.7 million Iraqis have left their homes, many in dire need of humanitarian care (to give a sense of proportion to the total population, this is equivalent to 10 million British or 50 million US citizens). Of these, more than 2.7 million Iraqis are displaced internally, while more than 2 million have fled to neighboring states, particularly to Syria and Jordan.[12]

The return of a few refugees from Syria and Jordan this year is not related to the success of the surge, the establishment of security in Iraq, or a reduction in "sectarian violence," the euphemism for death squads that have infiltrated the security services and local militias. According to the UNHCR, "only a small number have gone home, often because their resources are exhausted. Of those who returned to Iraq, many found their property occupied and suffered secondary displacement."[13]

In fact, international and Iraqi nongovernmental organizations (NGOs)[14] warned that the government should not ask refugees to return home as there were several cases of violence targeting Baghdad returnees, including the murders of entire families, but, "rather, the government should provide assistance to the displaced in the region, while working to establish the right conditions for returning Iraqi refugees, including security, essential services and effective means to resolve property disputes."[15] As Iraqi citizens, these refugees are the responsibility of the Iraqi government and of the provinces they have left, and should be cared for in an internationally agreed-upon legal and safe haven, especially as some host countries, such as Syria and Jordan, would be willing to cooperate with such guidelines.

DETAINEES

Since 2003, as many as 2 million Iraqis have been in US detention or have immediate family members in US detention.[16]

Mohammad Al-Dainy, an Iraqi parliamentarian, said recently that "there are at least 420 secret detention centres, in the country controlled by both the government and US-led foreign forces. . . . These centres of detention are completely illegal. Nobody can visit them. Conditions there are much worse than in official prisons."[17] The ICRC has access to only three sites under Iraqi government control.[18]

Most of the detainees in US prisons are men. Wives, daughters, and mothers of male detainees carry the burden of supporting their families and struggle to visit their loved ones. For a two-hour meeting with their detainee family members, they may have to take a perilous journey that can last several days.[19]

There is an indefinite number of female detainees. Shazha al-Ibosi, a member of parliament, and one of the very few Iraqi officials who admits the presence of women detainees, said, "There are 100 female detainees at Iraqi detention centres in Baghdad; 25 to 30 of them are under 18 years old."[20] On January 25, 2009, Minister of Women Affairs Nawal al-Samarrai said that women prisoners were routinely beaten, abused, and in some cases raped in both US and Iraqi prisons. Many women detainees have disappeared after being arrested by US and Iraqi forces, but because their families often do not report the cases, it is difficult to determine an exact figure for female detainees. Minister Samarrai added that political parties and militias hold sway over the courts and judges, thus prisoners often remain in prison indefinitely.[21]

Since 2006, it has become quite normal for Iraqi women to carry pistols when they travel outside their homes.[22] In fact, carrying arms seems to be an official solution to the dangers citizens face. In order to encourage the return of the 7,000 physicians who have fled the country, the government has decided to permit them to carry guns for personal protection. Dr. Ali Mahmoud, a thyroid specialist based on al-Kindi Street in West Baghdad, wonders: "What use will a pistol be to me if I am attacked by seven or eight gangsters in two cars carrying Kalashnikovs and PKCs [assault rifles]?"[23]

THE FUTURE

Barack Obama ran for US president with the promise of change in US policy towards Iraq. He vowed to withdraw US troops from Iraq in the first sixteen months of his term. However, there are already talks about how many troops should remain to provide security, train the Iraqi army, and defend Iraqi "democracy." Many Iraqis see this occupation as a continuation of the Bush team's colonial policy. After all, the withdrawal of US troops is part of what Bush had proposed in the security agreement between the US and Iraq. That proposed security agreement, along with the Status of Forces Agreement (SOFA), faced strong popular Iraqi opposition. Intended to legitimize America's presence long after the United Nations mandate for 154,000 troops in Iraq expired on December 31, 2008, it extends US forces' presence in Iraq to 2011, and subsequently extends the immunity of US troops, contractors, and mercenaries from Iraqi laws.

Iraqi resistance to occupation is on the increase, despite media reports to the contrary, and despite reduced US casualties in Iraq in 2008. History, including US history, tells of the grim fate of all colonial adventures. Most Iraqis see ending the occupation as the most urgent priority to regain peace in their country, but they are also looking for sober attitudes in the US towards its responsibility in this catastrophe. Those pondering the idea of change in the US must start looking at Iraqi people as equals, and must work together for a peaceful future based on equality and justice. Justice means making amends to the victims of the occupations and wars, taking responsibility for the damage to Iraq, from homes and schools, to roads and water plants. All the countries that participated in the war and in sanctions must take urgent action to help settle the millions of refugees and the displaced when they find their way home. "Prosecution of all those responsible for war crimes, human rights abuses, and the theft of Iraq's resources"[24] must be carried out.

Change must start with a solemn commitment to these basic principles, and a commitment to end all foreign interference in Iraq's affairs, including its oil industry, so that Iraqis can exercise their right to self-determination. We need to revive the international rule of law that would prevent a continuing cycle of violence and distraction. This is the change we need.

Haifa Zangana
February 2009

Introduction

This is a story written in exile, in the hopes that readers in the West will gain insight into a country they have impacted so fully and terribly. Writing this book is also a personal history that includes my story of growing up in Baghdad: living through wars and periods of peace and prosperity; joining movements for social change and participating in armed struggle; and working for equality as a woman, an Iraqi, and as a citizen of the world.

The US–UK catastrophic adventure has been shrouded by the old colonial phrase "liberators not conquerors," and by the new imperial lie of "establishing democracy." Both require the rewriting of Iraqi modern history, a process in which Iraqi people, women in particular, are often invisible or portrayed as victims. I have written this book to challenge this neocolonial misrepresentation. I hope there is also substance here for readers already wary of propaganda. I have tried to address the prevailing stereotypes of our history, society, and culture, and some of the misconceptions about the people of the Middle East. This is also an attempt to clarify how Arab and Muslim women, particularly in Iraq, continue to shape our modern history in response to the devastating situation they find themselves in due to external and homegrown challenges. It is a story of tremendous suffering and sacrifice, of courage and triumph, and also of hope and humanity.

Iraqi women have been among the most liberated of their gender in the Middle East. They have a long history of political activism and social participation since the nineteenth century, having taken part in the struggle against colonial domination and in the fight for national unity, social justice, and legal equality throughout the twentieth century. In fact, UNICEF reported in 1993, "Rarely do women in the Arab world enjoy as much power and support as they do in Iraq."

Nonetheless, as part of the misguided preparation for the US invasion of Iraq, Iraqi women had been selected to be the beacon of hope for all women in the Middle East. They were presented, along with the rest of our population, as needing to be liberated, despite the complex social history and systems in place in Iraq at the time.

Since the US-led occupation of Iraq in 2003, Iraqi women have conversely become confined to their homes, striving daily to survive the harsh realities of war and domination. A typical day for an average Iraqi woman begins with the struggle to get basic necessities—electricity, gas, water, food, and medicine—for herself and her family, and ends with a sigh of relief at making it through the day amid death threats, violent attacks, and kidnap attempts. Their political participation, if allowed at all, is reduced to bickering among a handful of "women leaders" over nominal political posts created under occupation.

Activism among women supportive of the US-led occupation has been redirected toward US-funded Iraqi women's nongovernmental organizations (NGOs) established in Washington, deemed necessary to engage "important voices which were missing from the debate—those of Iraqi women with personal experience of Saddam Hussein's oppression."[1]

This book will show that these NGOs are an integral part of the US strategy in Iraq. They have been influential in rallying support for the invasion and occupation, a role designed for them in the aftermath of September 11, 2001. Former secretary of state Colin Powell argued in his address to the NGOs in 2001 that "just as surely as our diplomats and military, American NGOs are out there serving and sacrificing on the frontlines of freedom. NGOs are such a force multiplier for us, such an important part of our combat team." Indeed, they represent US colonial policy rather than the interests of Iraqi men and women.

The blunders of the US administration in Iraq, this book further shows, may be located in this colonial policy, uninformed by a real understanding of the Iraqi people. The main misconception is to perceive Iraqi women as silent, powerless victims in a male-dominated society, in urgent need of sexual and political liberation. This image fits conveniently into the overall picture of the Iraqi people as passive victims who would "welcome the occupation of their country with flowers and sweets."[2] The United States confused the need of a people to get rid of a tyrannical regime with the right to impose a new colonial order. Their "women's rights" claims are mainly seen by Iraqi women as the second supply line of US colonial policy in Iraq, with NGOs, especially those oriented to women's issues, damaging the possibilities for the much-needed work by genuine independent women's organizations.

Writing this book has been difficult for two reasons. First, because it covers almost a century of Iraqi women's struggle for legal and social equality, and their attempts to overcome a multitude of obstacles. This struggle has been interrupted by political turmoil, two wars, sanctions, and the Anglo-American occupation which began in 2003. The United States labeled the occupation as "liberation" while grandstanding their support for "women's empowerment." In reality, Iraq now has US-sponsored medieval sectarian militias who have barbaric ideas about women's role in society. More drastic than earlier attacks on women's struggle, the occupation has left Iraqi women in a terrible state of regression.

Second, writing this book has demanded that I make sense of my forty years of personal involvement in Iraqi political and intellectual life both inside Iraq and as an exile. This has entailed celebrating Iraqi history, culture, and heritage, while at the same time recording the diverse and traumatic milestones shaping Iraq's modern history. So often this project has been overshadowed by news of the occupation's brutality, with its daily bloodshed and accompanying mayhem; it has been interrupted by phone calls from home about the displacement, kidnapping, and murder of relatives and friends. At times I have simply had to stop writing and wash my eyes, not daring to look in the mirror for fear of seeing blood.

Another challenge in writing a short history of Iraq is not to revisit ancient history. (In which case, this project would be neither concise nor published in a timely manner.) Most Iraqis, young and old, refer to historical events that took place a thousand years ago as if they happened only yesterday. This cultural tendency to take refuge in the distant past gains urgency at times of national crisis, under threat of foreign cultural domination and colonial rule. It is almost impossible not to see history as a living tradition and a component of our national identity when we grow up among thousands of archaeological sites, in a country that is often described by scholars as the cradle of civilization. As children we visit Babylon (2400 B.C.) in today's Babil province, fifty miles south of Baghdad on the Euphrates; we have family picnics near the arch of Ctesiphon (second century B.C.) in Taq Kasra, east of the Tigris, fifteen miles south of Baghdad, or in the city of Hatra (second century B.C.), capital of the first pre-Islamic Arab kingdom in the northern governorate of Ninawa.

For most Iraqis, there are two levels of understanding ourselves historically. The first is through ancient history, acknowledging our continuity from the time of Sumer and Akkad. The second is related to Islam, centered around Baghdad and the rise of the Abbasid in 750 A.D. Baghdad invokes creativity in literature, music, science, geography, philosophy, theology, and architecture—the full diversity of cultures that flourished in successive Islamic empires. When Abu-Jaafar Almansour built Baghdad in 762 A.D., it was a round city that embraced and developed the Islamic civilization to which non-Arabs and non-Muslims fully contributed.

I begin this book at the end of the nineteenth century, to highlight the emergence of the Iraqi women's movement as an integral part of the rise of Iraq's modern identity. A slow process of modernization was beginning to take shape while the country was still under Ottoman rule, and then continued in the fight against British colonialism.

The 1920s and the following three decades mark the rise of the modern state of Iraq. I argue that, contrary to the neoliberal view of our nation, Iraq is not an invented country, but has existed from time immemorial. Prior to the occupation and especially in its aftermath, there have been attempts by Western media and in academia to rewrite Iraqi history, in support of dismantling the Iraqi state. A common rationalization is that Iraq is an artificial entity concocted by British colonialism, whose constituents are at war with each other and need to be reconstituted. This is simply not true. From ancient times, Iraq has been a country straddling two rivers, the Tigris and the Euphrates. Over the centuries, boundaries of the outlying areas have changed in an irregular ebb and flow, and so have administrative centers and districts. But a central government has repeatedly risen in the region around today's Baghdad, to assert its power up and down the two rivers and their tributaries, because of an economic need for coordinated irrigation systems and the exchange of goods by river transport. It is worth noting that all the ancient capital cities of Sumer, Babylon, and Assyria are in the Iraqi territory, and that Iraq covers about three-quarters of the Tigris-Euphrates valley. The land making up the current country has been called Iraq in the languages of the ancient cultures of the region.[3] Within a radius of fifty miles of today's Baghdad lie Babylon and Ctesiphon, capitals of ancient Iraq. Within the same radius are also Kufa, Anbar, and Samarra, all capitals of successive Arab-Islamic states from the Middle Ages that controlled vast empires. Foremost among these capitals since its foundation in 762 A.D. is Baghdad itself, which in the Ottoman period ended up as the center of the three nominal provinces of Iraq, including Mosul on the Tigris to the north and Basra on the confluence of the two rivers to the south. The Mosul Vilayet, the former Ottoman province, included most of Iraqi Kurdistan.

These geopolitical facts form the background of a deep-seated and common set of customs and values among the population that make up the implicit civic codes of Iraqi society, however much that society is occasionally weakened by wars and disasters. And they must be taken into consideration in light of recent developments of the Iraqi state—its economy, oil industry, and health and education services, and the wider Middle Eastern politics within which current events are unfolding.

In this story of Iraq, I also present myself. I was in primary school at the time of the 1958 Revolution. An Iraqi girl with a Kurdish father from the northern city of Kirkuk and an Arabic mother who inherited the honorific title Alwiya[4] (my mother grew up in Karbala, one of Iraq's holy cities), I was raised between Baghdad, Kirkuk, and Erbil. My family's home in Baghdad was always crowded with our relatives from the northern cities. Khalil, my father, was fluent in Kurdish, Persian, and Turkish, but Arabic remained a closed book to him, and although he was a secular man he was proud to see me read and write in Arabic, the language of the Qur'an.

It was during the early days of the 1958 Revolution that I paid my first visit at age seven to Qasir al-Nihaya, the palace originally built for the Crown Prince Abdul Illah and called Qasir al-Rihab, which was opened to the public after the overthrow of the monarchy. That day, I went with my mother, two aunts, grandmother, and two brothers. We all wore our best clothes, like on days of Eid (feast). I remember the beautifully landscaped gardens. In the front yard there were stables. I complained about an uncomfortable pair of new sandals, but nobody took any notice. They were too busy looking, pointing, and whispering. I could not understand why we had to whisper; it was an empty palace after all. My grandmother at last took notice of my tears and scolded, "Be quiet, be quiet! We mustn't disturb the dead." Later, in the 1960s, the rooms were turned into cells where hundreds of Iraqis who opposed the Ba'ath regime, regardless of their religious or ethnic backgrounds, were tortured and killed. I was among those imprisoned there at the age of twenty-one.

In the aftermath of the 1958 Revolution, for the first time, ordinary Iraqi citizens owned the streets. This was a period of jubilation for women especially, with the revolution's constitution establishing legal rights for women, celebrating March 8 as International Women's Day and May 1 as

International Workers' Day with other free societies around the world. The thin layer of tribal, land-grabbing lords and the coteries of monarchical ministers imposed by the British (1932–58) evaporated into the Iraqi sunlight. We became the proud owners of our oil resources with Law Number 80, now enshrined as sacred in our collective memory as a symbol of independence. Our aspirations for a new life were as vast as our dreams.

In the early sixties, I joined thousands of women to demand the release of Jamilah Buhrayd, the young female fighter from the Algerian Resistance, who had been arrested by the French, imprisoned and tortured with others, among whom was the legendary Ahmed Ben Bella. The woman as fighter looms large in the Arab world. For us teenagers, it was Jamilah, not a pop singer or a supermodel, who served as our role model.

I retrace my own path with those of many others from this time period, demanding self-rule for Iraqi Kurds within a democratic Iraq, and joining the armed struggle to overthrow the Ba'ath regime within a movement stretching from Kurdistan to the southern Arab marshes.

I was one of many Iraqis who joined the Palestinian struggle following the 1967 War, believing that the occupation of Palestine and forcing Palestinians to leave their homes to live in refugee camps was simply a gross injustice that had to end. Like many of the supporters of their cause, we writers, journalists, artists, doctors, and students did not necessarily join their armed struggle, but participated in the ways we could. In Baghdad, I received training as a pharmacist, and was then appointed to manage the Palestinian Red Crescent's nascent pharmaceutical unit in Dummar, near Damascus. Palestinians relied mainly on receiving drug donations from international donors and countries such as China, therefore many of their most pressing health needs were not getting addressed and alternative health services were in high demand. In Dummar we tried to be self-sufficient, producing essential medications for the Palestinians living in refugee camps in Syria and Lebanon. But with severe budget restrictions and the high cost of equipment needed to manufacture drugs, it was an uphill battle.

Most of us did not have valid passports (this is an injustice common to Palestinians and Iraqis to this day) so we had to travel via the risky military route between Lebanon and Damascus in order to reach our depots and camps. Despite all the difficulties, we managed within four months to equip the factory with the required machinery needed to produce Paracetamol, aspirin, antacid tablets, cough syrup, and anti-diarrhea medication for children. Within a year, our drug factory became the flagship of the Palestinian Red Crescent, visited by many delegations. Our sense of achievement was great, as was our daily preoccupation with the future.

As some of these biographical details made their way into this book, I was faced with the difficulty of writing about the Ba'ath rule, from its rise to power in 1968 until its demise in 2003. This particular period invokes for me the images of tortured and executed friends (three of my close colleagues were murdered and a fourth, who was tortured, ended up in a mental hospital, and then, upon release, collaborated with the secret police), and the abuse and harassment of my family and me. After leaving Iraq late in 1974, my family had to report regularly to the security office to prove that they had no contact with me.

In order to understand the social, economic, and political changes that have affected millions of our people over thirty-five years of Ba'ath rule, I have had to look beyond my personal feelings to see its formative role in every aspect of Iraqi life, shaping the country and its people. The declared reasons for the invasion of Iraq by the US-British alliance were the existence of weapons of mass destruction, al-Qaeda connections with the Ba'ath regime, and the need to establish human rights, and in particular women's rights. All of these premises have proven to be false.

Indeed, the promotion of Iraqi women's rights as a justification for the invasion has proven to be the mother of all failures. Instead, Iraqi women have lost all they had achieved as activists before the invasion, and they comprise thousands of the 650,000 casualties, a number that has climbed since mid-2006.⁵ By mid-2007, one in eight Iraqis had left home to become a refugee, with up to 50,000 people leaving their homes each month. The United Nations Office of the High Commissioner for Refugees (UNHCR) has said that the exodus has been the largest long-term population movement since the displacement of the Palestinians after the creation of Israel in 1948. The Iraqi Red Crescent estimates that two-thirds of the displaced are women and children, often living in female-headed households. The Iraqi refugee catastrophe that only appeared in the media in early 2007 is the latest visible facet of the collapse of the US project in Iraq. This catastrophe is of a different scale and nature than the other aspects of that collapse, which include the rise in US and British military causalities, the exposure of systematic torture of prisoners and atrocities against civilians, and the escalating economic, political, and environmental costs of regional strategies implemented by the United States.

The forced displacement of two million Iraqis inside the country and another two million in neighboring countries has unfolded in stages, first as a trickle, then a flood. The latter, in 2006, followed a different form of "Shock and Awe": gruesome atrocities committed by murder squads and militias, which coincided with the occupation's quest for an alternative way to ensure US domination following its failure to subdue the country. The new strategy is based on fragmenting the population into manageable segments to be dealt or dispensed with.

In five years of occupation, the United States has moved from publicly opposing religious forces in the Arab world and advocating modern secular "model democracy" in Iraq, to open reliance on sectarian Islamist forces, a stark indication that it has failed to find any other social base for their new colonial domination. The United States has tried to justify this failure by claiming that the move to democracy initiated by the liberation exposed deep conflicts in Iraqi society that had been covered up by the previous dictatorships. Unheard of forms of violence, resulting in immense suffering for all Iraqis, is readily ascribed to sectarianism. We are being told repeatedly that the main story in Iraq is that Iraqis are killing Iraqis by the hundreds each day, and that the main question is whether it has yet become a sectarian civil war or not, and more recently, "Why do they hate each other?" Blaming the victims has become the widely accepted rationalization for foreign troops to remain in Iraq indefinitely.

The fact is that "dormant" sectarian tensions have been nurtured and funded through criminal gangs and neighborhood warlords. Not only have the occupiers been unable to control such explosions, they have destroyed Iraqi society's modes of coping with such problems themselves. The occupation has deliberately dismantled the state, army, and key structures of civil society so that people have been forced further back to the defenses of their smaller communities, which helped them during sanctions while the state still served as an overarching structure. However, these communities do not have inexhaustible resources, and their limitations were only manageable within the civil state. Control of organized gangs and massive corruption are problems an isolated community is ill-equipped to deal with. The communities struggle to prevent attacks and evictions of its members, often carried out under sectarian or ethnic guises by militias, unemployed youth, and those corrupted by the occupation. They also strain to contain the feelings of vengeance that follow atrocities against their fellow citizens. While many communities can withstand a great deal through local efforts, they need professional and civil society structures to endure the onslaught against them. But such personnel have been systematically evicted or physically eliminated since the occupation, and the communities have to fall back on deeper but weaker resources.

In fact, sectarianism is loathed by most Iraqis, and religion in general is perceived as a personal choice rather than a political tool of governance. Islam is part of one's culture and identity but never the one and only way of ruling Iraq. No wonder that the political parties wearing the religious turbans, be it Sunni or Shi'ite, or the ethnic robes, whether Kurdish, Tourkuman, or Yezidies, are failing to represent Iraqi people. No wonder that given the idea highly promoted by the occupation and its client regime that Iraqis hate each other, the testimony of Abu Ahmed from a displaced family does not reach the mainstream media: "My family is Shi'ite. We live together with a Sunni family. Both families were forced to leave their homes by militias. There are 30 of us, sharing the same living space: 14 children and 14 adults, including grannies on both sides. We live on an abandoned construction site and protect ourselves from the weather with plastic sheets provided by the ICRC [International Committee of the Red Cross] along with food supplies. The adult members of both families are trying to keep on working, taking any job we can find. But we don't earn enough to live decently."[6]

In the fifth year of occupation, the sectarian and ethnic divide between politicians, parties, and their warring militias has become monstrous, turning on its creators in the Green Zone and beyond, and not sparing civilians. One of the consequences is a major change in the public role of women. During the first three years of occupation, women were mostly confined to their homes, protected by male relatives. But now that the savagery of their circumstances has propelled many of them to the head of their households, they are risking their lives outdoors. Since men are the main target of US-led troops, militias, and death squads, black-cloaked women are seen queuing at prisons, government offices, or morgues, in search of disappeared or detained male relatives. It is women who have come to bury the dead. Baghdad has become a city of bereaved women.

Occupation has left no room for any initiative independent of the officially sanctioned political process, or for a peaceful opposition that could create networks to bridge the politically manufactured divide. Only the mosque can fulfill this role now. In the absence of the state, some mosques provide basic services, running clinics and schools, and caring for orphans.

In addition to the call to prayer, their loudspeakers warn people of impending attacks or appeal to blood donors. But these attempts to sustain a sense of community are regularly crushed.

Across the country, strands of resistance to occupation have developed, ranging from armed battalions to peaceful, political, and communal acts of dissent, increasing in extent and intensity. Many women are a part of this movement, providing direct and indirect support. Remember, armed resistance against occupation is a right under international law. And this resistance movement was born not only of ideological, religious, and patriotic convictions, but also as a response to the reality of the brutal actions of this occupation and its administration. It is a response to arbitrary break-ins, humiliating searches, arrests, detention, and torture. According to a recent report by the Red Cross, "the number of people arrested or interned by the multinational forces has increased by 40% since early 2006. The number of people held by the Iraqi authorities has also increased significantly." It is important to remember that the Anglo-American occupiers did not send to Iraq election monitors, the Royal Shakespeare Company, or planes dropping emergency aid. They sent the most powerful army equipped with the latest high-tech weapons, whether in the initial phase of "Shock and Awe" or at later stages using cluster bombs, phosphorus, a new generation of napalm called AK77, depleted uranium, and other unconventional weapons. In Baghdad alone, there are an estimated eight hundred hazardous sites, the majority related to cluster bombs.[7]

After five years of occupation, the US administration is still unwilling to admit that there are Iraqi men and women suffering appalling treatment as a result of the occupation, who are willing to fight for an independent, unified Iraq in control of its own resources, just as they fail to recognize that Iraqis are proud, peace-loving people, and that they hate occupation, not one another. Such Iraqi people are very different from the images the occupiers present at their PowerPoint-presentation meetings and briefings. Where tragedy in Iraq is admitted at all, it is talked about in terms of mistakes, and of problems among Iraqis themselves; not as a result of an illegal and immoral occupation.

How important is the women's perspective in this book? How specifically can we ascribe any issue as a woman's, whether in history or under occupation? It is of course impossible to separate the plight of women from the rest of humanity, but it seems to me that a women's perspective is relevant for three reasons. The first is related to human rights for women, as for all individuals, and how necessary it is for that right to be guaranteed and protected by law. Traditional patriarchal society, especially in the Arab and Muslim world, normally justifies strict gender roles as necessities for both family and community survival in a harsh world. The argument is that these roles, while restrictive for both males and females, better protect women and leave them revered as mothers, daughters, and sisters to a much greater degree than in modern Western society. While there is a certain merit in that argument, it denies the individuality of both males and females, and a glaring subordination of women is usually the price women have to pay for this protection and reverence. For these reasons women need an active civil society to delineate and protect their rights.

The second reason a women's perspective is critical has to do with gender-related violence. This is of particular importance at times of occupation, war, and armed conflict, often the context for sexual abuse of women and girls. Iraqi women under occupation, whether living with or without men, have been subjected to sexual abuse, torture, and death. According to an Iraqi member of Parliament, there were 1,053 cases of documented rape cases by the occupying troops and Iraqi forces from 2003 until early 2007. Women have been detained to intimidate or force their male relatives to admit to crimes that they haven't committed. There are over two thousand women detainees, some of them in custody with their infants, and others separated from their children, deprived of knowing their whereabouts.

The third reason a women's perspective is relevant relates to women as life-givers. Pregnant women need special prenatal and postnatal care, critical to keeping themselves and their babies healthy. In any one year, there are one million pregnancies in Iraq, one for every five households. This means that about half the households are either with pregnant women or with toddlers under two years old. Perhaps it can also be said that how a society treats its more vulnerable citizens is a litmus test of its humanity and its sanity.

That is the situation today. In the long view, there is a hopeful perspective for Iraqi women. The momentum of changes in Iraqi women's status in earlier decades, although violently interrupted by the sanctions of the 1990s and the present occupation, may well resume. The signs are that Iraqi women are not only taking part in the national resistance, and in actions to alleviate suffering and organize basic health and education services, but also are actively opposing sectarian politics and the fragmentation of their country. That is what will ensure for Iraqi women their future role in society as leaders of a liberated sovereign Iraq that combines national dignity, justice, and independent development with democracy and human rights.

I The Transition to Modernity

To understand the contemporary changes of civil society in Iraq, including the status of women within it, it is necessary to look at the rise of the modern state and the origins of the founding structures of the government, economy, and politics within which current events are unfolding. These structures themselves are deeply rooted in geographical, historical, social, and cultural influences that date back centuries.

The four centuries of Ottoman rule from the sixteenth to the nineteenth centuries provided a unifying power in the Middle East. In Iraq this meant having an overall structure for the scores of rural fiefdoms and township dynasties, maintaining irrigation systems, and dealing with warring tribes. It did not succeed in getting rid of tribalism, but reduced its most vile and violent effects. The Ottomans respected the traditional society and Arabic heritage and culture, except during the last few decades of their rule. They adapted a moderate school in Islamic jurisprudence, and their communitarian system of family and inheritance laws had a multi-cultural inflection that is relevant to this day. This system of cultural autonomy at the family and personal-property level allowed peaceful coexistence of traditional religions and sects, often intermingled in neighborhoods and towns.[1]

The British style of colonialism was another story. They began their occupation of Iraq in 1917 during World War I. They created the current state in a process that became known as the second fall of Baghdad, the first having taken place under the Moguls in 1258. (That fall and the fate of those who collaborated with the Moguls remains an emotional issue throughout the Arab and Islamic world.) Even though the fall of 1917 was not accompanied by as much destruction of the city as the first fall, it was still a great ordeal for Iraqis.[2]

Shortly after the occupation of Baghdad by British forces, General Sir Stanley Maude issued this proclamation: "Our military operations have as their object the defeat of the enemy, and the driving of him from these territories. In order to complete this task, I am charged with absolute and supreme control of all regions in which British troops operate; but our armies do not come into your cities and lands as conquerors or enemies, but as liberators."[3] The reality was different, despite the fact that in November 1918, the British and the French issued a declaration stating as their goal "the complete and final liberation of the peoples who have for so long been oppressed by the Turks, and the setting up of national governments and administrations that shall derive their authority from the free exercise of the initiative and choice of the indigenous population."

Britain and France split the Arab domains of the Ottoman Empire according to their strategic interests, dividing and conquering ethnic and geographic regions, primarily to prevent the emergence of strong new entities. Colonial rule and the division of Arab domains traumatized the still incoherent Arab elites, some of whom had naively turned against the Ottomans, though brothers in faith, and aided the British during the war by starting the 1916 revolt in Hijaz. Soon it became clear that the promise of a unified Arab free state and independence for the Kurds would be broken. The conflict led to solidarity among Iraqi elites with the public at large, including tribal leaders and religious scholars. Their shared disappointment and anger had been reported in the British media as early as 1919. A correspondent for the *Times* wrote on September 23, 1919: "I imagine that the view held by many English people about Mesopotamia is that the local inhabitants will welcome us because we have saved them from the Turks, and that the country only needs developing to repay a large expenditure of English lives and English money. Neither of these ideals will bear much examination. . . . From the political point of view we are asking the Arab to exchange his pride and independence for a little Western civilisation, the profits of which must be largely absorbed by the expenses of administration."[4]

The Kurds revolted in 1919 but were silenced by the same imperial power that promised them independence. Winston Churchill told the War Office (referring to the Kurds and Afghans): "I do not understand this squeamishness about the use of gas. I am strongly in favour of using poisoned gas against uncivilised tribes."[5]

On April 28, 1920, Britain was awarded a mandate over Iraq by the League of Nations, to legitimize its occupation of the country. The revolution of 1920 that followed led to a compromise of "independence under mandate" for Iraq as we know it today. Iraqis refer to the 1920 Revolution as *al-Thawra al-Kubra* (the Great Revolution); it united all Iraqis regardless of religion, ethnicity, or gender, against occupation and colonial rule.

The British restored control with great difficulty. First, they used Royal Air Force bombers against civilians and fighters, and then had to send for reinforcements from India and Iran. An estimated ten thousand Iraqis were killed.

The British deliberately muddied the ethnic waters by conforming border arrangements with Iran that cut across ethnic and linguistic regions, including parts of Kurdish areas despite promises of independence. They also tried to create a sectarian independent Basra but failed.

On August 22, 1920, T. E. Lawrence wrote an article about Iraq that could be easily mistaken for a commentary appearing in today's newspapers: "The people of England have been led in Mesopotamia into a trap from which it will be hard to escape with dignity and honour. They have been tricked into it by a steady withholding of information. The Baghdad communiqués are belated, insincere, incomplete. Things have been far worse than we have been told, our administration more bloody and inefficient than the public knows. It is a disgrace to our imperial record, and may soon be too inflamed for any ordinary cure. We are to-day not far from a disaster."[6]

In the aftermath of the 1920 Revolution, the occupation was replaced with a provisional Iraqi government, "assisted" by British advisers under the authority of the high commissioner of Iraq. The problems that ensued proved to be enormous. The British high commissioner had to devise a solution to reduce the loss of British lives and rising costs to the empire.

He did so by imposing a "suitable ruler." Finding one to install was not easy, but the British finally settled on Emir Faisal, the son of Sharif Hussain of Hijaz. To the British government, control of Iraq and its oil was a strategic necessity. But the Iraqi national liberation movements called for *Istiqlal al-Tamm*, "complete independence," which was seen by the British as "the catch word of the extremists here," and as an "idiot phrase which the extremists of Baghdad, and no one else, added to the referendum papers: cut off from the control of anyone."[7] Any protest against the British-imposed monarchy was regarded as the work of extremists.

The twenties were the formative years for today's generation in government and resistance. Many of the same family names of the twenties crop up in the media now.[8]

For many Iraqis, the US-led occupation in 2003 is practically and emotionally analogous to the 1917 British occupation of Iraq. The Iraqi collaborators of the US proconsul Paul Bremer chose June 30, the date of the first battle of the 1920 Iraqi Revolution, to announce their advisory Interim Governing Council. The United States looked to the 1920s for instruction when events did not turn out as they and their allies had expected. The head of the occupying authority's Tribal Affairs Bureau admitted that he had been relying on a 1918 British report in his attempts to make sense of local politics.[9]

■ ■ ■

The emergence of the Iraqi women's movement was an integral part of the construction of Iraq's modern identity, which began to take shape while the country was still under Ottoman rule and which continued while it was fighting British colonialism. Muslim reformists, together with intellectuals who included early Marxists and poets, were venturing on a new path. They were trying to stretch the boundaries of education and knowledge in order to overcome the apprehension associated with the

West and other foreign ways of thinking. Some intellectuals called for the education of women to enable them to participate in building the nation; others tried to accommodate traditional ways of thinking by advocating the liberation of mothers of future generations in order to educate their otherwise ignorant children.

Throughout history, poetry has traditionally been the dominant literary genre in Iraq, and a powerful tool for conveying political messages. Poets have often enjoyed prestigious positions as spokesmen for their tribes, emirs, sultans, or modern rulers. Therefore, in order to understand the political and social changes in Iraq, and the women's liberation movement in particular, it is essential to look at the role played by poetry in both its oral and written forms. Generations of Iraqi women have used the oral tradition of poetry as an educational tool to complement the Qur'an in teaching their children history, morality, and responsibility. Women recited poetry during the 1920 Revolution to encourage fighters against British occupation. It is no coincidence that the first calls for the liberation of Iraqi women were initiated by poets, both men and women. Poets were more adventurous. They called upon women to burn their veils (which covered the face) and abayas (traditional Iraqi cloaks).[10] But conservatives, women included, were ready to defend tradition as a symbol of honor.

Socially and culturally, Arab poets, writers, and intellectuals were expressing new ideas for change and searching for national identity. One of their main arguments was that a national liberation struggle should earn women their rights. In 1899, in his book titled *Tahrir al-Mar'a* (*The Liberation of Women*), Qassim Amin, an Egyptian lawyer, was the first to call openly for women's liberation. He, like most pioneers, argued that women's liberation was a patriotic duty that would serve the whole of Egypt, not just its women. "The evidence of history," he wrote, "confirms and demonstrates that the status of women is inseparably tied to the status of a nation."

Amin criticized some of the practices prevalent in Egypt and other Muslim societies under Ottoman rule at the time, such as the veil and women's segregation, which he described as un-Islamic, or contradictory to the true spirit of Islam. With this combination of patriotism and his reinterpretation of Islam, he laid the foundation for future reformist critics of such practices against women throughout the Islamic and Arab world. He also established an acceptable language of revolt used by many Arab and Muslim postcolonial feminists.

The official version of the history of the women's movement in Iraq claims that men were the first feminists, thereby linking the movement to the early Arab women's movement, especially in Egypt, Syria, Lebanon, and Tunis. However, written history often ignores many aspects of women's achievements, as they were mainly expressed orally. Poetry, songs, folktales, and lullabies were often not recorded, and subsequently are unrecognized and ignored. There were at least twenty female poets who were active in the 1920 Revolution against the British occupation.[11] At the end of the nineteenth century and beginning of twentieth century, Iraqi men and women had reached that moment in history when social change was bound to happen. However, without the genuine yearning of women to change their status, there would never have been a women's liberation movement.

Jamil Sidqi al-Zahawi (1863–1936), a poet, was interested in science and philosophy. He was the first to call for women's education and unveiling as early as 1904, and by 1923 he had helped his sister Asma al-Zahawi to publish *Layla*, the first Iraqi women's magazine. He earned many enemies and his life was threatened several times.[12] Ma'ruf al-Rusafi (1875–1945), a poet, journalist, and member of Parliament, wrote extensively about the sufferings of Iraqi people and their struggle for independence.

Both poets revolutionized the public discourse of women's issues. They highlighted particularly a woman's right to education, work, and choice of husband, and led a revolt against what they called rotten norms and customs. They were careful not to blame religion, but rather critiqued traditions for discriminatory practices. In fact, they often presented women in Islamic history as role models for courage and leadership in society. They considered the veil and abaya as signs of backwardness that did not befit Muslim women. Al-Zahawi wrote several poems calling on women to get rid of their "dark shrouds," to tear them off and burn them whether they be veils or abayas. Al-Rusafi blamed Eastern women's veiling and lack of education for the backwardness of the East.

The fact that they were both from highly regarded religious conservative families gave them creditability to raise these sensitive issues, although this did not stop some conservatives from threatening their lives. [13]

In advocating socio-religious reforms, they both sought the liberation of society as a whole, not just that of women. Al-Rusafi, in particular, spoke out against the British occupation and British-controlled monarchy, and made the correlation between the need to liberate women and society and the need for liberation from imperial domination. As a result, he was labeled a communist by the monarchy.

Um Nizar (1908–53) is considered a pioneer in calling for women's liberation, establishing identity and pride in Arab nationality, and fighting colonialism and injustice. Her real name was Selma Abdul Razaq. She chose to publish her poetry under the pseudonym Um Nizar (mother of Nizar, the name of the eldest of her seven children), as it was and still is the custom to address mothers or fathers not by their first names but as mother or father of their first child, out of respect. (Nazik al-Malaika, her daughter, who became one of the most important poets and critics in the Arab world, chose differently.)

Um Nizar's first poem was published on April 14, 1936. Her husband, Sadiq al-Malaika, a poet, Arabic-language teacher, and the editor of a twenty-volume encyclopedia on grammar and literature, insisted on sending it to the Baghdadi newspaper, *al-Subh*. She had written the poem in memory of al-Zahawi and his support for women's liberation. It was published immediately and received wide acclaim. Her only book of poetry, *Songs of Glory*, was published by her daughter twelve years after her death.

Um Nizar's poetry addressed Arab national identity, her pride in its history, and the struggle against the occupation of Palestine, all of which became dominant themes in Nazik's poetry as well. In advocating Iraqi women's emancipation, she challenged women to regain their role in society by reminding them first of their glorious history and of their achievements in the fields of science, literature, and war. Secondly, she compared her past with her present subordination, a life forced upon her. Thirdly, she called on women to break free from the chains of tradition, to wake up from their long sleep, warning them not to waste their time in silly consumer traps but to study and work hard.

Another source of pressure for women's liberation came from the emergent Left. The whole of the Middle East had been influenced by the 1917 October Revolution, which stood for self-determination of nations while also espousing women's rights and the socialist alternative. The first Marxist feminist in Iraq was Husain ar-Rahhal, a student at Baghdad's school of law, who studied in a high school in Berlin at the end of the World War I and traveled to India. He was influenced by the rise of communism, and in 1924 he formed the first Marxist study circle in Iraq. It published *As-Sahifa* (The Journal), which appeared from 1924 to 1925, then again briefly in 1927, and called for Iraqi women to be freed from their ancient fetters. But in assailing tradition in this one realm, it soon found itself up against a force that permeated every structure of society. This was, of course, the religion of Islam as interpreted by the traditionalists then. The journal was not deterred, however, and proceeded to question Islam's very foundations. This was more than traditionalists who dominated public opinion could take, and *As-Sahifa* was shut down.[14]

While these pioneers were engaged in public arguments about the status of women, Iraqi women were moving at their own pace, slowly but surely, making their way into the public domain. Their early struggle can be seen in Iraq's public schooling, in the media, in early women's organizations, and to a lesser extent in political life.

In 1899, the first general primary and secondary schools for girls were established. Ninety girls were enrolled. From that date until the late 1950s, state-run schools were opened side-by-side with Mullah and Kitab (religious classes often attached to a mosque), especially in rural areas.

We must not blame tradition and religion solely for families' lack of enthusiasm in sending their children, especially girls, to school. There were few opportunities for general education, and schools were neither affordable nor available. Poverty and the lack of schools built under occupation were major factors that prevented families from getting their children educated.

Most schools opened in Baghdad, while most other cities and towns had no schools at all. Education, especially at the secondary and university levels, was for the urban elite. Children of affluent families whose parents enrolled them in private, missionary or religious schools (Jewish schools, for example[15]), received a better education and therefore stood a better chance of working in the government. Children in primary school were rarely able to continue their studies.

Like in any other country in the world, daughters and wives of the upper classes were the first to gain access to public life. In the case of Iraqi women, daughters of ex-officers from the Ottoman ruling class were the first to be educated and to graduate from public universities. Men and women who were sent off for a European education became a new elite. Schooling in this period (1914–39) was still mainly confined to those who could afford it[16] or possessed some other advantage. But it was still limited by the reluctance of society to send children to school (sons, but even more so daughters), which would alienate them from their families and traditions, and by the reluctance of foreign rulers to educate a class which could not be absorbed into government service and might therefore form an opposition.

Qebul, women-only gatherings in private houses, can be seen as the base from which women's charity organizations emerged in Iraq. They were very popular among middle-class women, providing them with a chance to see one other, discuss news, gossip, eat, exchange ideas about the latest fashion and recipes, and arrange marriages. They also offered support to women and families in need. Depending on the interests of the women involved, women's "receptions" were either a base for a progressive campaign or little more than a social outing. *Qebul* were still popular in the main cities of Iraq as late as the 1970s.

Iraqi women began their public social activities through "The Society for Women's Awakening," which was established in 1923 by a group of daughters of former Ottoman officials and officers, some of whom belonged to prominent urban families.[17] The Kurdish Women's Foundation was founded in 1928. Charity organizations established by wives of officials and ministers aimed to provide protection for children, especially orphans. The Iraqi Red Crescent was established in the mid-1930s. These organizations generally combined raising awareness with charity, teaching handicrafts such as sewing and tapestry, and combating illiteracy.

Journalists and writers contributed to the debate on women's status and education. Rafaiel Bati published *al-Huriya* (Freedom), a newspaper, in 1924. It dealt mainly with literature and paid great attention to translations, free verse, and support for women's rights. Its well-balanced coverage of women's issues attracted people's attention and sympathy.

In October 1929, *al-Bilad* newspaper published the first "Safhat al-Sayidat Wa al-Banat" (Women and Girls Page), which appeared every Saturday. It was one of the first to specifically deal with women's daily issues and what they had to face in demanding their rights and education.

Women writers contributed to the page using pseudonyms. Here is an excerpt from one of the published articles: "Dear sister, what are you thinking of now and tomorrow? Tell me. Haven't you been hibernating long enough in this deep sleep, which led you to the utmost labyrinths of darkness and degradation? Haven't you had enough of your laziness? Ah, my heart is about to break, to shatter at this plight. Rise up and start working for your dear homeland. Take a look at the daughters of Turkey, your neighboring country, who are always enthusiastic for nationalism armed with science and faith."[18]

Layla, the first Iraqi women's magazine, was published on October 15, 1923. Edited by Paulina Hassoun, it appeared every month for two years. Many Iraqi and Arab writers and poets contributed to the magazine, which covered the status of women, art, literature, and home economy.[19] Faced with protests from conservatives, it was forced to close.

■　■　■

In 1932, Iraq was declared an independent state and a member of the League of Nations, but only after signing a new treaty that allowed the British to retain their power through military bases, advisers, and the control of oil, and as the coordinator of foreign policy for the next twenty-five years. Iraqi forces had to be trained by the British, and arms were to be provided. Certain Iraqi groups and parties supported the British in their policy, hoping as time passed they would achieve a greater degree of self-governance. The British strategy was to protect their own interests through agreements with local governments, so that they would maintain ultimate control without the responsibility for regional issues. Not surprisingly, another popular uprising broke out against the oppressive regime of the monarchy, which had failed to understand the depth of feeling among Iraqis against occupation. In the years that followed, many opposition leaders were executed and thousands more were imprisoned. Elections were manipulated and force was used against popular demonstrations.[20]

The cost of living was high, poverty was widespread, and corruption rife. In 1935, hundreds of members of the Yazidi minority group were arrested, six were hanged, and the rest imprisoned. Bombing and military force were used against popular uprisings. Military coups d'état and more popular uprisings followed, all demanding significant social and political reforms.

In 1941, the Iraqi government refused to allow passage of British troops through Iraqi territory and declared its support for Germany in the Second World War, acts that led to the Anglo-Iraqi War and the reinvasion of Iraq by British troops. Women took part in demonstrations in 1941 and 1948, to protest against the signing of a new binding agreement between the monarchy and the British government, during which demonstrators were shot at by the police. These demonstrators included Zakia Shweliya, who became the first female martyr. She was called Fatat al-Jiser (Girl of the Bridge), as she was shot near one of Baghdad's bridges. Two women, Souad Khairy and Amida Misri, were arrested and given life sentences.

In the 1948 al-Wathbah uprising against the Treaty of Portsmouth, angry people took over the streets.[21] Hundreds of women took part in the demonstrations; many of them were arrested. This was followed by the 1955 uprising against the Baghdad Pact (a treaty signed by Iraq, Turkey, Britain, Pakistan, and Iran, pledging economic and military cooperation) and the 1956 uprising in support of Egypt's nationalization of Suez Canal. In the aftermath, King Faisal II declared martial law and suspended the parliament. Between 1921 and 1958, Iraq had an astonishing thirty-eight cabinets, some of them only lasting twelve days. The mainstay of a corrupt and docile regime was the presence of British forces on the ground.

Iraq joined the Arab League in 1948 and participated in the first Arab-Israeli War. The occupation of Palestine and Britain's role in the establishment of Israel, despite the fact that 90 percent of the native inhabitants were Arabs, together with the failure of Arab governments to act decisively, dominated the political and social landscape in most Arab and Muslim countries, including Iraq, and would continue to do so for generations to come.

The issue of Palestine, together with the 1920 and 1958 Revolutions, became the three most important factors in determining and shaping modern Iraqi identity. All were concerned with fighting occupation.

Socially, the monarchy gradually became alienated from the people and a serious impediment to the progress of the Iraqi economy as a whole. In the end, the economic growth of the country did not help the monarchy. Its moral alienation from the masses was fatal, and it could no longer count on the loyalty of the officials, the army, or the police for support.[22] Still, this period saw the opening of opportunities for girls' education and the entry of women into professional spheres and government employment. All of this was eased by the growth of oil income.

Control of Iraq's oil was a necessity for the British Empire. In fact, oil had been a strategic factor behind European interest in Iraq before the outbreak of World War I, ever since surface deposits had become visible in the north of the country. The Ottomans had plans for its development with the help of the Germans and the British. These included a project for a German railway line to the Persian Gulf, with prospecting rights on either side of the line. In 1927, huge oil fields were discovered near Kirkuk in the north, which brought relative economic improvement. Exploration rights were granted to the Iraqi Petroleum Company (IPC), which, despite its name, was a British oil company. For Iraqis, oil became economically important in the 1930s, gradually becoming another arena for the struggle against colonialism. Direct income to the Iraqi state from oil rose in the 1950s as a result of the increase in oil production by the IPC, a step that was taken to punish Iran for daring to nationalize its oil in 1953. In 1952, a new agreement with Great Britain gave the IPC greater control over the country's oil, and a greater share of oil revenues. The IPC ran its affairs totally independent of the rest of society and the national economy, keeping tight control of oil knowledge and skills. Until the revolution of 1958, Iraq had neither a college department nor any scholarships in the fields of oil geology, engineering, or economics. As a result, there was great antipathy toward the company, giving rise to slogans such as "Arab oil for Arabs," and later driving the movement for nationalization. Such sentiments also led to a more protectionist stance by regimes in the Arabian Peninsula who feared claims on their wealth by poorer Arab countries in the name of pan-Arabism.

There was an increase in the number of students registered in public schools, but the ratio of male to female students remained problematic.[23] Poverty and the unavailability of schools, combined with traditional attitudes toward girls and the belief that boys were the future breadwinners, reflected badly on girls' education.

A report by the Ministry of Education for 1955–56 indicated that there were 1,748 primary schools, 261 of which were for girls, and 152 secondary schools, 45 of which were for girls. The number of students in 1956 was 252,732 male and 79,949 female. At the level of higher education, there were 3,000 male students and 1,205 female students.[24]

Most female teachers, like those in the 1920s, were daughters or wives of MPs, ministers, or leaders of political parties. However, despite the slow process of expansion of the school system, the introduction of modern education hastened social changes especially for women, which provided them with the tools to fight poverty and helped them rise to positions of professional importance. Above all, it helped to erode the traditional divide between the public and private, providing women a gateway to public life.

It is worth noting here that Iraqi women, like women in any other traditional society, had enjoyed the freedom to visit extended family, relatives, and neighbors. For women of my mother's generation, visiting crowded temples, shrines, or mosques on a religious holiday was always a good excuse to wear her abaya and go out. Obviously, leaving home daily to go to school was different. Getting an education became the defining act of establishing women's place within the public domain. Still, on the eve of the 1958 Revolution, more than six-sevenths of the population were illiterate.[25]

Progress in health care was also limited. In 1950, there were 403 clinics and 71 hospitals in the whole of Iraq, of which 11 were private. These provided 4,900 beds, 2,000 of which were for female patients only. (That's one bed for every 1383 women.) There were only three maternity hospitals in the whole of the country, with a mere 200 beds. There were 811 registered doctors in Iraq in the same year, 444 of whom were based in Baghdad. Given these facts, it is easy to understand why people felt so furious with the monarchy, especially after the increase in oil revenue.

Closely linked to the issue of attending public schools was the issue of dress code. At the age of thirteen, sometimes earlier, girls had to wear the abaya, but not cover their faces, when they went out. With schools came the increase in social interaction between girls and women of other faiths and backgrounds from outside their immediate neighborhoods, and as they compared their situation with what they were learning about the modern world, they felt encouraged to fight for education and unveiling, in some cases more fiercely than men did. Usually education preceded unveiling, as veiling was regarded among students as a form of female servitude.[26] Girls enrolling in high schools and colleges in Baghdad during the 1930s and '40s continued to wear the Iraqi abaya over European clothes.

According to some histories, in the early 1930s the first Iraqi woman to unveil was Majda al-Haidari, wife of Rauof al-Chadirchi, though others mention Aminah, sister of ar-Rahhal, as the first.[27] In any case, both women were from well-established, affluent families. From that point on, some discarded their abaya when entering college, though some women chose to wear the veil, and others had to, as their parents would object if they did not. Social changes varied from one city to another, and from the city to rural areas, though women in rural areas did not wear the abaya if they had to work in the fields.

In Baghdad, there was a more rapid pace of change than in other large cities, such as Mosul or Basra, but in general it is true to say that women's liberation remained the idea of a few urban, intellectual, reformist elites. It was only after 1958 that it became a real movement.

Aminah, sister of Husain ar-Rahhal, was the first Iraqi woman to become a member of the central committee of the Communist Party, serving from 1941–43. The Communist Party called continually for the liberation and empowerment of women, which would enable them to participate in the national struggle. In 1938, Aminah attended the first Women in the East conference in Damascus and helped to establish the Arab Women's Union.

In 1944, a group of women applied for a license to form the Iraqi Women's Society against Fascism.[28] The group aimed to raise awareness among women regarding their rights and to highlight the dangers of fascism to humanity. They also established links with the outside world, participating in the International Women's Conference in Copenhagen in 1946, and joining the Women's International Democratic Federation. The same year witnessed the dismissal and arrest of Habiba Musha'al, one of three female students at the college of engineering, who became the first female political prisoner. More and more women became active in various political parties and organizations, and by 1952 there were 150 female political prisoners.[29]

The Society for the Defense of Women's Rights was founded in May 1952 and constituted in effect the women's organization of the Communist

Party. It changed its name in 1959 to Iraqi Women's League. A branch of the society was established in the Kurdish area in 1953.

There is a need to document the unofficial aspects of women's non-public political activities, characteristic of traditional societies, especially during periods of political violence and intifadas. In this respect, Iraqi women were actively involved in delivering messages, distributing leaflets, transferring weapons, hiding printing equipment, and caring for the wounded, as well as supporting their male relatives and families especially during their imprisonment. Women also established the Red Crescent Society and the Society for Protection of Children and Motherhood. This was followed by the efforts of other political parties to establish women's organizations such as the Muslim Sisters' Society and the Union of Iraqi Women. All of them reflected the same principle: in fighting alongside men, women were also liberating themselves. This was proven in the aftermath of the 1958 Revolution that ended the British-imposed monarchy, when, within two years, women's organizations had achieved what they had failed to during thirty years of British occupation: legal equality.

■ ■ ■

On July 14, 1958, a group of officers from the Iraqi army with links to a broad front of political parties overthrew the Hashemite monarchy, and ended forty years of British domination of Iraq. The "Free Officers" captured Baghdad's radio and TV station, and proclaimed a republic. Within hours, the streets where teaming with crowds of ecstatic supporters. The officers gained control of the country with virtually no opposition, in what is still referred to as the revolution of the 14th of July. The July 1952 military coup in Egypt had already been christened as a revolution through similar mass support. Revolution was in the air at the time throughout the region after the Bandung Conference of nonaligned nations heralded a new route for a postcolonial world.[30]

For the great majority of Iraqis, the revolution provided a chance for a fresh start. Doors that were previously closed to them were opened. Both the poor and the middle classes took to the streets and demonstrated jubilantly against all symbols of colonial and collaborative politics.

Revolutions are hardly well-organized or coherent events, and the July 14 Revolution was no exception. Positive changes ensued alongside bloody disputes and fragmentation. Most Iraqis agree that its achievements outweighed the failures. The socio-economic developments that took place in the few years that followed the revolution were worth the pains that accompanied it.

Under the leadership of Brigadier Abdul Karim Qasim (1914–63), head of the Free Officers, and his associate Colonel Abdul Salam Arif, a wide range of reforms were introduced. The revolution came to symbolize a brief moment in Iraq's modern history that united all Iraqis against a hated regime. For many Iraqis, Qasim's regime, with its education, housing, and land reforms, signified a golden age that was greeted with great popular enthusiasm and support. Dreams were abundant, expectations high. Streets became colorful with noisy demonstrations and celebrations.

It was also a time when politics, perhaps for the first time in centuries, belonged to the people: to the poor and illiterate, riddled with trachoma and bilharzia, suffocated by traditions and religion. Politics was no longer the private property of the elite. Qasim was loved by poor people as an icon for the revolution, and he addressed them publicly, often for hours.

The short-lived revolutionary period, which ended with a bloody coup in 1963, achieved what decades of British mandate, the monarchy, and over four hundred years of Ottoman rule had failed to provide: a degree of stability and security, which Iraqis built on their own.

The very first statement of the 1958 Revolution, known as "Manifesto Number 1," summarizes its aims and vision, and can be read as an indicator of most of the subsequent political, economic, and social change. It draws a line between the needs and desires of the Iraqi people and those of foreign governments, oil corporations, and their allies. The statement declared the country a member of the group of newly independent third world nations: "The affairs of the country must be entrusted to a government emanating from the people and working under its inspiration. This can only be achieved by the formation of a popular republic to uphold complete Iraqi unity, to bind itself with bonds of fraternity with Arab and Muslim countries to work in accordance with UN principles, to honour all pledges treaties in accordance with the interests of the homeland, and to act in compliance with the Bandung Conference resolutions. This national government shall be known from now on by the name of the Iraqi Republic."[31]

Following the revolution, the principle source of conflict among its leaders and on the streets was not its social agenda but centered on the identity of Iraq itself. Iraq was part of the Arab nation, "but not part of a part," Qasim said, when he refused to join Nasser's then newly formed United Arab Republic of Egypt and Syria. The concept of Arab nationalism which underlay the 1958 unity between Egypt and Syria was used by the Ba'athists and pan-Arab nationalists to oppose the Communist Party, which supported Qasim. Soon foreign powers joined in the struggle, the issue of Kurdish independence was raised, and schisms appeared that have divided Iraqis politically ever since, continuing now under occupation. However, political affiliations based on class struggle and economic gains, rather than religious, sectarian, or ethnic issues, were, and still are, the yardsticks by which Iraqi internal conflicts should be judged, however much the waters are muddied by identity politics.

Within fourteen days of the revolution, the Interim Constitution was published. It declared that all Iraqi citizens were equal under the law and granted them freedom without regard to race, nationality, language, or religion. It stated for the first time that "Iraq formed an integral part of the

Arab nation," and that "Arabs and Kurds are partners in this homeland." Islam was declared the religion of the state. The government freed political prisoners and granted amnesty to the Kurds who had participated in the 1943–45 Kurdish uprisings. Exiled Kurds returned home and were welcomed by the government.

On the eve of 1958, it was apparent that regarding women's status, traditional society in general could accept a public and even influential social role for women, but only in high-status professional domains. Of course, similar values applied to men, since professional jobs had always been valid substitutes for noble birth. Still, major changes were taking place. Women's participation in the national struggle alongside men paid off. The Personal Status Code was issued in 1959, which granted women equal rights on many levels. It established a uniform set of laws governing family and married life. In this respect, it was the most advanced family law in the region, as it granted women greater rights in areas such as inheritance, and it limited polygamy. Naziha al-Dulaimi, head of the League for the Defense of Women's Rights, was appointed as a cabinet minister, the first female cabinet minister in all Arab countries.

Education was in mass demand. New schools were built. Some young women joined the People's Resistance Force, a youth organization attached to the Communist Party to defend revolution, an unprecedented activity in Arab countries that was frowned upon by traditional society. Civil society was gaining power. Trade unions, women's organizations, and student unions were established, and classes were held to eradicate illiteracy.

The jurisdiction of tribal sheiks over their communities was abolished. Land reforms were introduced restricting the size of estates and redistributing the once communal land. For the first time in centuries, farmers became owners of land they worked. Laws to control residential rents were also introduced.

There were radical but measured moves over the issue of sovereignty. In 1959, Iraq withdrew from the Baghdad Pact and from the sterling zone.

Negotiations over Iraqi oil prices between the Iraqi authorities and representatives of the British-owned IPC took place in Baghdad between August and October of 1961. When the company failed to meet Iraqi demands, the government passed Law Number 80, by which Iraq regained control of all the unexploited areas of oil in Iraq, 99.5 percent of the total. This arrangement significantly increased oil revenues accruing to the government. Qasim announced the establishment of an Iraq National Oil Company (INOC) to exploit new territory.[32]

Cultural activities in Iraq also flourished in the first three years of the revolution. Many international works of literature were translated into Arabic and published in Iraq for the first time. In one year during the revolution, the total number of books published exceeded the number of books published in the thirty years before the revolution.[33]

At times, the issue of women's rights was relegated to a secondary position, even by progressives; in the anticolonial struggle, liberal or Left political movements formed alliances with nationalist forces that upheld traditionally conservative views on women's issues. For example, very few public political meetings and demonstrations were mixed, since the traditionalists opposed it, and even the clandestine cell structures in the Communist and Ba'ath parties were segregated until the 1960s.

The conflict between the communists and the pan-Arabs, with their international and regional alliances, seeped gradually into civil society, creating a partition that would separate Iraqis for years to come. Women's organizations were attached to these political parties, inevitably used as propaganda swords in the bitter ideological battle. Women of the Republic, which was established by the Ba'ath Party to challenge the popularity of the League for the Defense of Women's Rights, was busy promoting the party's program, while the latter was pressing for the Communist Party's unequivocal support for Qasim's leadership.

Ideological labels, whether communist, nationalist, or Ba'athist, were the abayas that covered all cultural aspects and activities, including fiction writing, research, art, poetry, and literary criticism. Two prominent women poets of the period, Nazik al-Malaika (1923–2007) and Lamiah Abbas Imara (b. 1929) reflected this ideological schism at its very beginning under the republic. To a certain extent, they can be seen as representative of the women's movement and its struggle through two different approaches.[34]

Nazik al-Malaika composed her first poem in classical Arabic at the age of ten. She studied literature at the Higher Teachers' Training College in Baghdad and later at Princeton University in the United States. In 1947, she published her first collection of poems, *Night's Lover*. In 1949, her second collection, *Splinters and Ashes*, was published, with a preface that introduced free verse as a new form of poetry that neither follows a strict metric system nor a particular rhyme scheme, thereby challenging centuries of classical form. This revolution in verse, shared with poet Badir Shakir al-Sayyab, aimed "to seek a greater freedom which would enable the poet to realize an organic unity in his work, a fusion of form and content."[35] Nazik and Badir's influence was soon felt in the entire Arab world. With her husband Abdel-Hadi Mahbouba, Nazik helped found the University of Basra in the south of Iraq in the 1960s. Nationalism and social issues were an important component of her poetry. She wrote about the occupation of Palestine, the Algerian Resistance against the French, and the defeat of the Arab armies in the war against Israel in 1967.

Nazik was also a strong advocate of women's liberation. Her two lectures from the 1950s about women's position in patriarchal society, "Woman between Passivity and Positive Morality" (1953) and "Fragmentation in Arab Society" (1954), are feminist classics. Her poem "Lament of a Worthless Woman" might well represent her views on this subject. But it was her poem about Jamilah Buhrayd that greatly influenced my generation. Jamilah, a young Algerian girl who as a teenager fought against the French occupation of her country, was imprisoned and tortured by the French, and became known throughout the Arab world as a hero of the Algerian Revolution. When Algeria gained its independence in 1962, Jamilah was released. The poem conveys the feeling of anger at the betrayal of Jamilah by the world. It is also a good representation of the historical commitment of Iraqi writers and poets to social and political issues.

JAMILAH AND US[36]

Jamilah! Beyond the horizon, far beyond the borders of nations,
    you weep.
Your hair loose, your tears soak the pillow.
Are you really crying? Does Jamilah cry?
Don't they give you music and song?
Didn't they make offerings, of words and more words to you?
So why the tears, Jamilah?

The details of your torture were on every tongue,
And that hurt us, it was hard for our sensitive ears to bear.
You were the one imprisoned and shackled
And when you were dying for a sip of water,
We marshaled all our songs
And said, "We'll sing to you, Jamilah, through the long nights."
All of us said: They gave blood and fire to drink.
All of us said: They put you on the cross.
But what did we do? We sang, we praised your heroism, your
    glory.
We made promises, false promises, drunken promises,
And we shouted, "Long live Jamilah! Long live Jamilah!"

We fell in love with Jamilah's smile.
We adored her round cheeks.

The beauty that prison had gnawed away at revived our love.
We were infatuated with her dimples, with the braids of her hair.
Did we not use her suffering to give meaning to our poetry?
Be silent before this noble suffering.

Their intent was evil. They cut her with sharp blades.
We gave her smiles, good intentions.
They hurt her with knives.
We, with the best of intentions, hurt her with ignorant, uncouth
    words.

The teeth of France tore her flesh.
She was one of us, our kin,
And the wounds we inflicted are more painful to bear.
Shame on us for all the suffering of Jamilah!

Lamiah Abbas Imara graduated from the Higher Teachers' Training College in Baghdad in 1950 and went on to work as a secondary school teacher. Her father's death when she was young tinged her poetry with long shadows of sadness.

In an article entitled "I and My Abaya," she deals sarcastically with the problems associated with wearing the full veil. She described its ugliness, its depressing color, and how it restricted women's movement. Above all, she blamed the abaya for the stagnation of literary life in Iraq. As expected, the article caused a stir among the conservative circles in Baghdad, but earned Lamiah immediate support from the Left.

In her first book of poetry, Lamiah defiantly wrote about love and seduction. One of her famous love poems is "If the Fortune-teller Had Told Me." It ends with these two stanzas:

If the fortune-teller had told me

My lover would bring me the sun in his hands in the
Icy night
My lungs wouldn't have frozen
And the troubles of yesterday wouldn't have been
Magnified in my eyes.

If the fortune-teller had told me
I would meet you in this maze
I would have wept for nothing in this world
But kept my tears
For a day you might abandon me.[37]

Lamiah's poetry dealing with social and national issues, in particular the occupation of Palestine, was very powerful. In her poem "Palestine," she appeals to all Arabs to work together to liberate the occupied land, and conveys the historical importance of the Palestinian issue in our lives. It was a priority for pioneer women poets, despite their engagement with family life, women's liberation, and their different political affiliations. It continues to be so.

While Nazik became famous for her pan-Arab inclinations, Lamiah was associated more with the Left. Both would suffer under future wars, oppression, and sanctions.

On June 28, 2004, in his farewell message to the Iraqi people, Paul Bremer, the US-appointed ruler of Iraq, recited these words by the ancient poet Ibn Zuraiq al-Baghdadi:

I bid farewell to a moon in Baghdad
That rises over the skies above al-Karkh
Although wishing to part with life's serenity instead.[38]

Like other occupiers in history, Paul Bremer thought that by reciting Iraqi poetry he could show his understanding of Iraqi society, history, and culture. He failed to understand that those who occupy a country can never reach the deep foundations of the people whom they are "defending and protecting" at such a high cost. Fearing for his life, Bremer left Iraq in a hurry.

■ ■ ■

On the February 8, 1963, I woke up to the sound of gunfire; it was the first Ba'ath coup. I watched with my family, through a small window overlooking an alley, as young men with machine guns took control of the streets. I was twelve years old and it was the first time I had witnessed anything like this scene. Our Fedhil area was in the center of Baghdad near the defense ministry. Tanks were parked around the ministry and other public buildings nearby, and streets were closed to traffic. The fighting between Ba'ath party members and pan-Arab nationalists on one side, and the communists and soldiers defending Qasim's regime on the other, went on for a few days.

Normal radio and TV programs were replaced with military music and hymns. Schools closed; university students went on strike. The whole country descended into chaos as the outbreak of violence became inevitable. The Ba'ath party was in the process of taking control of the country from Qasim and the communists. Hundreds of people were killed in the fight and in detention. Estimates vary but their numbers run into the thousands.

The new government was made up of Arab nationalists. Under Colonel Arif (the coleader of the July 14 Revolution), who was not an extreme ideologue, were the Ba'athist army chief Ahmed Hassan al-Bakr and the Ba'ath Party secretary Sa'di.[39] This government lost control after less than ten months. The regime's unpopularity—due to the atrocities carried out by the Ba'ath militia, infighting, tensions between Iraqi national interests and incoherent pan-Arab nationalist projects, and their inability to crush the resurgent Kurdish rebellion—soon led Arif to abandon the Ba'ath Party in November 1963 and to leave power solely in the hands of army officers under his leadership and that of his brother Abdul Rahman. The Ba'ath Party had showed itself to operate more like a gang than a political party. Furthermore, the majority of Iraqis regarded it as a group contracted by the CIA and Kuwait to overthrow the national government and assassinate its patriotic leader, Qasim.[40]

The most enduring image of the ten months during which the Ba'ath Party held power was of the notorious militia, the Nationalist Guard, which terrorized, imprisoned, tortured, and executed Iraqis, women included. Those crimes stained the Ba'ath Party's reputation for years to come, to a much greater extent than mob scenes of early 1959 did to the Communist Party's image. A clear distinction emerged between the Ba'ath Party and the moderate, less ideological Arab nationalists who largely upheld the law, though in a patriarchal manner.

Arif led the Iraqi government into the pan-Arab camp, forging a close relationship with Nasser, and actively considering unity with Egypt and Syria. When Arif was killed in a helicopter crash in 1966, his brother Abdul Rahman assumed leadership. He was a quiet, unambitious man, unusual in the Iraqi political arena at that time. Iraqis enjoyed political and social stability under the two Arifs, which led to an era of relative freedom celebrated by many writers, artists, and poets and known as the "Golden '60s." But the renewal of conflict with the Kurds transferred power increasingly away from central government to various army factions.

■ ■ ■

On July 17, 1968, the Ba'ath Party under the leadership of al-Bakr seized power again. A Revolutionary Command Council (RCC) was formed.

Saddam Hussein, who by 1969 had become the most important Ba'ath party official, came to be known as Mr. Deputy. On July 16, 1979, al-Bakr stepped down and Saddam replaced him to rule Iraq until the US-led invasion in March 2003.

The Arab Ba'ath Socialist Party (the word Ba'ath translates literally as "resurrection" or "renaissance" in Arabic[41]) began as a secret group of nationalist intellectuals formed in 1940 in Syria by Salah al-Din al-Bitar and Michel Aflaq. They were middle-class educators who were influenced by Western schooling and sought to establish a secular Arab nationalist party. Towards the end of 1943, the name "Arab Ba'ath Party" was adopted and the party participated in the resistance against the French and later in the Palestinian war of 1948.[42]

Underlying the Ba'ath ideology was a perceived need to reassert the "Arab spirit" in the face of foreign domination, and to regain Arab pride. Moral and cultural deterioration, it was felt, had so weakened Arabs that the idea of Western supremacy spread throughout the Middle East. Arabs needed regeneration, a sense of the common heritage of people in the region to drive off these debilitating external influences.

Significant expansion of Ba'ath ideas beyond Syria's borders took place only after the Palestinian war of 1948, when lack of Arab unity was widely perceived as responsible for the loss of Palestine to the colonial settler state of Israel. By 1950, the party had branches in almost every Arab country. The Iraqi branch was established in 1954, and took on the new name of Arab Ba'ath Socialist Party.

It created a one-party system in which (except for the period of the Progressive National Front [PNF] with the Communist Party, 1974–79) it controlled all political appointments, economic policy, cultural activities, and foreign relations, using political campaigns to eradicate what it called "harmful pre-revolutionary values and practices." It built a system of police control that showed little tolerance for those opposing their views, and it aimed to enforce the one ideology of "Pan-Arab Unity, Freedom, and Socialism."

This one-eyed perspective, combined with power, arrogance, ruthlessness, and the need to build a nation, was the base upon which the policy to shape Iraqi women's lives, family, and society took place over thirty-five years.

Events took a tragic turn following Saddam's rise to power. The two main periods of this history are 1980–88, when Iraq was at war with Iran, and 1990–2003, the sanctions years.

The Iran-Iraq War was to challenge Iranian dominance in the Middle East, undermine the appeal of the revolutionary Shi'ite regime, and end the dispute over the Shatt al-Arab waterway. It was the longest, most devastating war in modern history, and led to over a million deaths on both sides. Thousands of Iraqi Shi'ites allegedly of Iranian origin were forcibly displaced.

Early in the war, Iraq's French-built nuclear reactor was destroyed by an Israeli strike, leading Iraq to develop its own secret nuclear power. The regime's anti-Israeli stance has remained implacable.

Throughout the war period, the two main Iraqi Kurdish parties, Kurdistan Democratic Party (KDP) and Patriotic Union of Kurdistan (PUK), allied themselves periodically with the regime or with Iran to gain effective control over parts of northern Iraq. The regime launched counterinsurgency in 1987–88. Effectively much of Iraqi Kurdistan was a theater of war between Iraq and Iran, with several hundred villages destroyed and massive relocation of people into strategic camps. One campaign, called Anfal, literally "spoils of war," terrorized villagers and led to claims of use of chemicals, mass graves, and to massacres like that in the border town of Halabja in March 1988. The regime thrived on fear to subdue the population, and its later denials of mass graves and ascribing the Halabja massacre to the Iranians carried little weight.

The Arab Gulf States saw the Iran-Iraq War as a defense against Iranian ambitions, but then turned on Iraq, with Kuwait suddenly demanding return of funds that had been understood as gifts. That led to Iraq's 1990 invasion of

Kuwait, then to the US-led first Gulf War on Iraq in 1991, which was followed immediately by drastic UN sanctions. Thus began the fragmentation of the country, especially through the imposition by the United States and Britain, rather than the UN itself, of no-fly zones to prevent the regime from using its armed forces in the north and the south.

Thirteen years of sanctions were imposed by UN Security Council resolutions in 1990–91. These required Iraq to surrender weapons of mass destruction and allow full UN inspections. Iraq maintained that it had complied, but its response was deemed inadequate, so further resolutions maintained a very severe sanctions regime. This was only modified in 1996, taking the form of the Oil-for-Food Programme allowing Iraq to sell oil to buy its own products under UN-controlled distribution. This program provided minimal relief to a population that had for six years lost 90 percent of its income.

During the sanctions, the two main Kurdish parties reasserted control over parts of northern Iraq patrolled by the United States and Britain as a safe haven. Civil war between the PUK under Jalal Talabani's leadership (president of Iraq at present) and KDP under Masoud Barazani's leadership (president of the regional Kurdish government) broke out in 1994. Barazani asked Saddam Hussein for help against Talabani, which he happily provided. However, the bitter fight between the two parties, which caused the killing of about five thousand Iraqi Kurds, only ended in a US-sponsored agreement in 1998.

■ ■ ■

The lives of three generations of Iraqis have been shaped largely by the Ba'ath regime.

Events took a dramatic turn following its coup of 1968, and a tragic turn with Saddam Hussein's rise to power as supreme leader eleven years later. Two opposite attitudes dominate writings of that period. One demonizes the Ba'ath regime and Saddam (from outside Iraq); the other eulogizes them (mostly from inside Iraq).[43] One places blame for all the calamities that befell the country on a fascist regime with a messianic leader. The other shows it as one chapter of a heroic struggle against the historic enemies of Iraq, Arabs, and even Islam.

Writing objectively or comprehensively about those thirty-five years of Ba'ath rule is not easy. It is well known that the regime discouraged social and economic research, and in times of war any independent research into the economy was prohibited. Access to facts and figures was limited, and one had to go through official channels to get them. For information on the status of Iraqi women, one had to go through the official women's organization called the General Federation of Iraqi Women (GFIW). There are few studies dealing with women's social status and development available covering these thirty-five turbulent years.

Furthermore, in the aftermath of the 2003 invasion, in addition to the initial looting and burning of books, people were too scared to keep books that featured Saddam's photograph or that dealt with his regime, despite the fact that every official publication under Saddam had to include his picture. It wasn't good enough to tear up the occasional photo or single page, and then save the books and magazines; under occupation, a book could be confiscated during violent arbitrary raids and considered a deadly "terrorist" weapon. People have been forced once again, just as they were under the Ba'ath regime, to burn books. The De-Ba'athification Committee, set up under the occupation, has directed the last blow to anyone hoping to understand the period through independent research and historical documentation.

In May 2003, Paul Bremer, the head of the US-established Coalition Provisional Authority (CPA), issued CPA Order Number 1, De-Ba'athification of Iraqi Society, to purge members of the former ruling Ba'ath Party from public life. Ahmed Chalabi, known as one of the sources for US intelligence about Iraq's weapons of mass destruction capability that has since proven to be a lie, was appointed as the head of the committee. The formation of the committee was considered by many Iraqis to be a tool of revenge and an abuse of power. Bearing in mind that almost all Iraqis were members of the Ba'ath Party (voluntarily or out of political necessity), we can see the extent of the damage that resulted in applying the CPA order. The committee's name (the Arabic word used is *Ijtithath*, which means uprooting) has come to symbolize the terrorizing of ordinary people, depriving them of their livelihood while encouraging informers and corruption. More than sixty thousand public service employees lost their jobs; twenty-eight thousand of them were teachers. The CPA order was essentially a weapon in the hand of officials vying for positions within the ministries, and has been used to tarnish the reputations of political opponents within the parliament itself.

While it was presented abroad as an orderly process similar to the de-Nazification in Germany after World War II, in Iraq it worked more like a witch hunt. Mithal al-Alusi, a member of the committee and an old associate of Chalabi's, justifies the nature of his mission, saying, "It's true, Iraq was held hostage by the Ba'ath Party, and most people had no choice but to join. Our job, however, is to root out those who don't want to see any change happening in the new Iraq."[44]

The committee ordered a purge in Iraqi universities of all books, documents, papers, publications, and unpublished theses, accusing them of being "un-academic" in their research on Ba'ath's ideology and the glorification of its leader.[45] Thus we are deprived of much-needed information about the social, economic, and political changes that have affected hundreds of thousands of our people over decades. Without a thorough and nuanced understanding of our history, we are destined to repeat our mistakes.

In writing about this period, I have had to force myself to face *my* enemy, the Ba'ath regime.

I was on my way back from Nasiriya, in the south, to my family home in Baghdad, when I was arrested for my involvement in the Iraqi Communist Party and for my role in armed struggle while I was a student at the school of pharmacy at Baghdad University in 1972.

During the first two weeks of interrogation, I was kept in a cell next door to the main torture room. There I heard screams that I could barely distinguish as human. For two weeks, I could not sleep, listening by day for the torturer's steps to approach my cell and take me to be interrogated again, and by night trying to recognize the voices of the tortured, so as to discover who else had been arrested.

I was the last within my group of four to be arrested. By the time I was brought in, they had already been tortured and had confessed.

Survivors of torture and interrogation are often kept in prison to be humiliated and to be "taught a lesson." In my case, I was kept for six months. My Kurdish relative Sabah Mirza, the personal secretary and bodyguard of Saddam Hussein for over twenty years, intervened on my behalf because of my parents' persistent appeals to secure my transfer from Qasir al-Nihaya to Abu Ghraib prison, especially as I was the only female detainee there. And holding a female detainee, at the time of "peaceful" negotiations between the Ba'ath and Communist Parties to establish the PNF, was not politically correct for either party. Above all, I owe my life to my parents who did everything possible to publicize my arrest and imprisonment, and to my mother in particular, who refused to give up hope that I was still alive.

Every day she went to the Ministry of Defense. At the rear gate, there was an information office dealing (nominally) with political prisoners. My mother had one activity: to leave home early each morning with a cardboard box containing a towel, some clothes, sanitary towels, and tins of food. To the officer in charge, the sergeant, and soldiers, she would repeat the same request: "Take the box. My daughter needs clothes. She was not allowed to take anything with her when arrested." The answer was always the same: "We haven't got a prisoner here with that name. Who said we have political prisoners? Don't you know we are living through a new era, the era of the National Front?"

The second week, my mother no longer questioned the officer. She began taking her youngest daughter along and the two of them sat in front of the Ministry's gate. Sweating in the baking sun of August, covered with her abaya, my mother was seen by every person who went into the Ministry, morning and afternoon. Her presence provoked whispers and inquiries. Many people avoided looking at her, at her box. One day a soldier approached and asked, "Khala [Auntie], why are you sitting here?" Before she had the time to answer, the sergeant shouted at the soldier to leave her alone, not to interfere.

The third week, the officer ordered the sergeant to get rid of her. He managed to move her away from the gate. The next morning, my mother and sister took their place a few meters away. At the end of the third week, the sergeant called her: "What's your daughter's name? Give me the box. Go home." She gazed in awe at the cruel face with its thick moustache, handed over the box and began to cry. At home, though, she was able to smile and exclaim to my father, who was filled with anger and bitterness, "Didn't I tell you? She's still alive!"

The irony is that thousands of mothers just like my mother continue to queue for weeks on end at the gates of prisons, detentions centers, and military camps in "liberated Iraq," waiting for any news about their loved ones.

■ ■ ■

The Ba'ath Party's second rise to power led to its thirty-five-year rule, the longest reign for any political party in the history of modern Iraq. It played a formative role in every aspect of Iraqi life. All previous parties and regimes were subject to regional and international influence. The communists blindly followed the Soviet Union's policy. Documents released after the collapse of the Soviet Union proved that many of their leaders were on the payroll of the KGB. The Ba'ath Party was closely allied at various times to the CIA, Britain, Egypt, Syria, and the Soviet Union. The pan-Arab nationalists were largely dependent on help and advice from Egypt's Nasser. The Islamist Al Da'wa Party had direct connection to Iran, while the Kurdish nationalist parties have often been linked to the CIA, Israel, and Iran.

None of Iraq's political parties have a clean hand in the calamities that have afflicted the country since the revolution of 1958. What makes the Ba'ath Party more responsible than others was its control of state power for so long, and its relationship with the United States during the Iran-Iraq War, which had a terrible impact on the Iraqi people and the region in general.

There is a perception that the advancement of women's rights under the Ba'ath Party, with its leading role in women's education and its promotion of women in professions, was in part due to the necessity brought about by wars, but was also a form of "state feminism." I find both notions misleading.

At times, the Ba'ath Party presented itself as a vanguard in progressive causes. At other times, it made simplistic claims misrepresenting women's achievements in Iraq as a kind of state feminism that was forcing the pace of modernity on a reluctant society. My own experience and that of many Iraqi women in the second half of the twentieth century belie this notion. Iraqi society generally placed girls' education high on its list of priorities, and encouraged them to be active in life. I can still hear my father's voice telling me time and again whenever he noticed my involvement in political activities: "Get your degree first, then do what you like." For some women, education and work had become the essential tool to defy class, segregation, tradition, and poverty. This applied even to conservative Muslim families, though they may have preferred separate schools for their adolescents.

In 1970, old Khairullah Talfah, Saddam's uncle and mentor who was appointed the Governor of Baghdad, tried to impose a strict dress code on youth. He issued an edict allowing the police to paint the legs of any young woman found to be wearing a miniskirt. The edict was soon relaxed, then abandoned due to the insistence of students (I was one of them) to wear what they liked. The Ba'ath regime did not want to be seen as holding back Iraqi society. The regime carried within itself the same pressures as society at large, and was largely responsive to social preferences. At times of affluence this went one way, and at times of trouble it went another.

When we examine the Ba'ath strategy towards Iraqi women, we will see that, being a secular socialist party, it was almost a mirror reflection of Soviet-style policy as adopted by the Iraqi Communist Party (ICP), with its women's organization, the Iraqi Women's League (IWL). There was one major difference. While the Communist Party's role models were Soviet women and their achievements, the Ba'athists looked toward historical Arab women's achievements and, in the 1990s, when the solidarity of the Muslim world was needed, to Muslim women's achievements.

Both parties believed that women's liberation could not be achieved without national liberation from colonialism and reactionary forces, and that women's emancipation was part of the nation's advancement. But most Iraqis did not recognize how much they had in common, because the two parties despised each other's ideologies and denied the existence of any similarities in theory or practice.

Examining two texts—the first which was written by Fahad,[46] general secretary of the Communist Party in 1944; the second, a speech by Saddam Hussein in 1972—there are surprising similarities, which lead me to believe that Saddam not only read Fahad's text, but was significantly influenced by it, a notion that completely contradicts his party politics.

Fahad outlined the communist vision of the emancipation of Iraqi women, which was to become the blueprint for all members of the party, the IWL in particular, until the collapse of the Soviet Union in the 1980s and the re-branding of the ICP as neoliberal, keen to join the occupation under a sectarian quota.[47] This has also been reflected in the IWL, which re-branded itself as an NGO working to fit within the political process imposed by the occupation to "depoliticize" women's issues.[48]

Though the ICP had only a very short period of indirect power (1958–63), I believe it had a major influence on women's lives since 1940. Fahad compared Iraqi women with "her Soviet sisters," and he saw the emancipation of women to be part of the revolutionary model:

> The principal enemy confronting any woman who seeks a change in her way of life and liberation from the accumulated servitude of centuries, is the same enemy who confronts changes in the way of life of her people and their liberation. This enemy is the foreign power and its two internal supporters: backwardness and reactionary customs which are wrong for our current generation.
>
> The most important task which falls on the women's movement in Iraq today is to join in the national liberation movement, the struggle for democratic rights.[49]

As deputy of the Iraqi President, Saddam Hussein outlined a similar Ba'ath strategy towards Iraqi women in his speech titled "Women: One Half of Our Society": "The commitment to the Revolution and the defense of its ideals and gains, together with the maintenance of the interests of the toiling masses, are the only way to the liberation of women. . . . The Arab Ba'ath Socialist Party sees women's role as essential in a noble and prominent role in our people's struggle for freedom from imperialism, dictatorship and reactionary regimes and for achieving the pan-Arab aims of unity, liberty and socialism . . ."[50] Like Fahad, he saw the struggle for women's rights as part of the larger struggle for solidarity across ethnic lines: "It cannot be a genuine revolution if it does not aim at the liberation of woman and the development of her material and cultural conditions.

"The Arab women, together with their Kurdish sisters and all other women of Iraq, are capable of following a correct path and playing their pioneering role in the construction of the revolutionary society."

Contrary to the ethnic and sectarian spin by the US and the UK to justify the invasion, the Ba'ath Party was a secular party influenced by socialist ideology and had close links to international Left movements. It stressed the national identity of the people as Iraqis and had no ethnic or religious slant. The media story today about a fundamentalist Sunni Arab Ba'ath Party is baseless. In fact, Ba'ath founders in Iraq have mostly been from Shi'a backgrounds in the southern Iraqi provinces, the same as for the majority of the party's membership till the invasion of 2003. In pursuit of its national identity policy, Ba'ath census reports and other official documents did not generally give the religious, sectarian, or ethnic composition of the population. They also refrained from identifying prominent personalities by their surnames if those denoted religion, sect, or ethnicity.

■ ■ ■

In the 1970s, the Ba'ath regime nationalized the foreign oil companies,[51] and Iraq finally gained complete sovereignty over its most valuable natural resource. Money was abundant, and most of the oil wealth was invested in developing the oil industry; construction and industrial projects; housing and agricultural programs; education and health services; and cultural programs, festivals, and international events.

As part of the overall social and economic development, there were genuine advances for women's rights in education, employment, and in cultural terms. The 1970 Constitution affirmed the "equality of all citizens before the law regardless of their religion, language or sex." The Constitution directed the state to eliminate illiteracy and to ensure the right of citizens to free education, from elementary school through to university level, while also guaranteeing equal opportunities without discrimination.

However, the Constitution also granted the party's Revolutionary Command Council (RCC) extensive powers, followed later by further modifications granting Saddam Hussein, as a head of the RCC, even more control.[52] Equal opportunities for work had been an important part of the regime's policy to improve women's status, therefore various legislation was enacted, such as Labor Law Number 151 of 1970, which reduced women's working hours during pregnancy and granted them the right to feed their babies, and an amendment to the Civil Service Act Number 44 of 1977, which stipulated that women have the right to a fully paid seventy-two-day pregnancy leave.[53] Other legislation followed. Men and women were to receive equal pay for equal work. Women working in the government sector were entitled to a one-year maternity leave, receiving their full salary for the first six months and half salary for the next six months. A wife's income was recognized as independent from her husband's. She had the right to acquire and dispose of agricultural land.

In 1974, education was made free at all levels, and in 1979 it was made compulsory for girls and boys up to the age of twelve. These legal enactments provided a solid framework for the promotion of women and the enhancement of their role in society. They had a direct bearing on women's education, health, labor, and social welfare.[54] In addition to building nurseries attached to women's workplaces, measures were also taken to ensure women's access to opportunities in non-traditional fields of employment.

Women's right to vote in national elections was declared in 1967. This was extended to the right to be nominated as candidates in 1980. State policy during the 1960s and '70s strongly supported the creation of extensive and well-distributed physical and social infrastructure. Public services, including an extensive network of well-equipped and well-staffed health facilities, ensured wide and equitable access of the population to health care. Drugs, medical supplies, and equipment were amply provided as needed by the health facilities. The Iraqi health system was probably one of the best in the Middle East.[55]

At that time people in general were willing to compromise their freedom of speech, press, and independent political organizations for improvements in the economy, health, education, and their social lives. The Kurds, who wanted complete autonomy, were partially pacified with the March 11, 1970, agreement allowing self-rule. Most opponents to the Ba'ath regime among writers, poets, and Communist Party intellectuals were gradually accepting the leadership as a version of the "noncapitalist way," with hundreds returning to their official positions from which they had been purged earlier. That followed the liquidation of the independent faction of the Communist Party, which had not forgiven the Ba'ath its earlier policies and collaboration with the CIA in the 1963 bloody coup, and the period of terror and violence wrought by its National Guard, which Iraq had never seen before.

I was a member of this faction, the Iraqi Communist Party–Central Leadership (CL), when I was imprisoned in 1972. The CL was a revolutionary faction in the Iraqi Communist Party that emerged in the mid-1960s. It opposed the ICP policies of collaborating with governments associated with the Soviet Union. In the late 1960s, the CL turned into a powerful group within the ICP, which advocated armed struggle in an effort to raise the masses, inspired by the Cuban revolution and the struggle in Vietnam.

The CL saw the rapprochement between the United States and the Soviet Union as imperialist bargaining at the expense of third-world struggle. Our goal was to overthrow the Ba'ath military regime and to support the liberation of Palestine and the right of self-determination of the Kurds within a unified democratic Iraq. What was meant by democracy was not based solely on the electoral process but rather on economic policy aiming to establish equal rights for the masses.

In the first few months after the Ba'ath coup in 1968, the regime dealt a heavy blow to the CL. Most of the leadership was captured and killed under torture, and a few prominent ones became collaborators.[56] Khalid Ahmed Zaki, an exile who returned to Iraq to lead a group of young communists in armed struggle, was killed during action in the south. I did not meet him personally because I joined the CL group after his death, but, like many young Iraqis, I had been influenced by his revolutionary ideas and life, which restored hope in the future of the struggle against the military Ba'ath regime and the pro-Soviet Communist Party. Khalid for many of us had the aura of Che Guevera.[57]

Khalid was among the thousands of Iraqi government-scholarship students sent after the 1958 Revolution to the best universities around the world to study engineering and science. Those graduates were to play a crucial role in the rapid technical and intellectual development in Iraq from the 1970s onwards. Khalid led the Iraqi Student Association in London and was a researcher at the Russell Foundation. On returning to Iraq, he formed the Revolutionary Cadres group within the ICP, and organized an armed-struggle group in the deprived Marsh-Arab areas in the south. He applied the principle that the revolution is to be conscious and instigated rather than an event that matures through vague dynamics.[58]

Inside Iraq, a few CL cells continued to operate well into the 1970s, consisting mainly of workers and university students. I was part of one of them, a group of independent dreamers who continued the underground struggle to overthrow the Ba'ath regime, dressed in the traditional abaya that provided the invisibility needed when traveling away from main cities to remote rural areas, from the mountain villages in Kurdistan in the north, to the Arab marshes in the south. At times, I had to pass through dozens of checkpoints. Being a woman in traditional dress in the rural areas made me the perfect courier between three groups. One was in Baghdad, where I was in charge of the women's organization and a member of the central students' committee; another in Kurdistan, where a base with a dozen comrades was established near the village of Nawchilican; and a third group in the Arab marshes, near Amara, in the south.

Nawchilican was the military base where I met scores of fighters, some of them staying permanently, others like myself who came for a brief period, either to be trained or to bring weapons and leaflets and receive instructions. It was a place of enthusiasm, of dreams of a better world, in a country enveloped in fog. It attracted young people clamoring for an independent Iraqi movement working for a better future.

Very little has been written about this chapter of Iraqi struggle, its martyrs, and its spirit of idealism. This gap continues on the two sides of the ICP, even those opposing the collaboration with the occupation, people who still look at the struggle in terms of infighting within the party machine, or who trivialize the CL because of its youthful constituency. The few survivors of the CL are oddly silent, as though the survivor guilt were too much to break through.

The Baghdad and southern groups were subsequently killed, many executed at Abu Ghraib; the northern group suffered infiltration, paranoid infighting, shady deals with Kurdish leadership, and finally folded with the collapse of the Kurdish revolt in 1974.[59]

At this time, the pro-Soviet communists took part in the Progressive National Front government with encouragement from the Soviet Union, who had signed a treaty of friendship with the Ba'ath regime. The situation was more complex, however, than the fact that the Ba'ath Party had a monopoly of power. Iraqi people's attitude towards the party, its leadership, and particularly Saddam Hussein, was never straightforward. The foundations were being laid for promising development in Iraq. A sense of affluence and a rapid rise in the standards of living prevailed. The regime's support for the Palestinian people and its close link with international Left movements forced the few intellectuals who continued to criticize the regime's oppression of dissidents, along with its torture and suppression of freedom of speech, into exile.

Steady political development was soon to be disrupted. The government took advantage of the inter-Kurdish divisions between Talabani and Mulla Mustafa al-Barazani to challenge the historical leadership and policy of the Mulla. The Kurdistan Democratic Party (KDP), siding with Iran, was persecuted, and its leadership forced into exile. The communists were routed out from government, with some imprisoned or killed and thousands fleeing the country. The 1970s ended with the Iranian Revolution, the rise of political Islam, a fear of an Iran-Syrian axis, and Saddam Hussein taking over all power in a bloody internal Ba'ath coup. All these events took place during the peak of Iraqi economic development.

■ ■ ■

There has always been tension at the state level, as well as close ties on a social level, between Iran and Iraq, rooted in a mix of geography, culture, and millennia of history. But in modern times, Iraqi nationalists—whether under monarchy or the republican front of the 1958 Revolution—thought of Iran as a threat. Iraq blamed colonial British policy, which arranged for Iran to annex the strategic oil-rich, Arabic-speaking Khuzestan province at the mouth of the Gulf—a region that had been part of Iraq's Basra province. This caused a stranglehold, together with Kuwait, on the only sea access to Iraq for a landlocked area with a distinct language. And Iran had continued to refuse finalizing border demarcations, especially alongside the Shatt al-Arab waterway.

Iraqi and non-Iraqi nationalists united against Iran under the Shah, who was a pillar of American policy and an open ally of Israel. Iran conspired against the republican Iraq with the remnants of the monarchic regime and cynically used Kurdish nationalist leaders against Iraqi governments. In response, Iraq supported opponents of the Shah including

Ayatollah Ruhollah Khomeini, the future leader of the Islamic republic, who was based in Najaf and was freely operating for fourteen years, up to a few weeks before the Iranian Revolution. The Ba'ath regime started to deport people of Iranian descent, and to confiscate their property. In the increasingly paranoid atmosphere, thousands of Iraqis were seen either as security threats working for the Iranian regime directly, or as a social base for undesirable Iran-leaning religious authorities. The deportations led some Iraqis to support the 2003 US-UK invasion, many of whom were the offspring of those deported to Iran by the Ba'ath.

Rapid changes in the Iran-Iraq relationship started to happen in the 1970s. In order to crush a mounting Kurdish uprising that threatened oil fields with Iranian artillery, Saddam Hussein surrendered to key border demands of the Shah on the Shatt al-Arab. The Kurdish revolt collapsed overnight, and Iraq and Iran started working together in OPEC. Soon thereafter Islamic agitation started to grow in Iran, the United States sided with human rights groups there, and in 1979 the Shah was toppled. The Iranian Revolution, however, had created Islamic momentum, which now posed a radical and militant threat to the Iraqi regime and that of other Arab regimes. The Arab world split, with Syria and Libya siding with Iran, and Iraq joining the anti-Iranian block, however much they differed in their approach to the West and Israel.

Khomeini believed that the oppressed Shi'as in Iraq, Saudi Arabia, and Kuwait could follow the Iranian example and turn against their governments to join a united Islamic republic. Saddam's secularist, Arab-nationalist, Ba'athist regime was seen as un-Islamic and "a puppet of Satan," and Khomeini called on Iraqis to overthrow it. What followed was a dramatic bloody attack on the shrine of the holy city of Mecca in Saudi Arabia, and the start of Jihad against the newly arrived Soviet forces in Afghanistan. Soon thereafter arose a worldwide rivalry involving the Saudis espousing a fundamentalist Sunni Islam to counter Iranian influence. Saddam Hussein, faced with an alliance between Iraq's two neighbors Iran and Syria, assumed full power that year. Iraq started lodging complaints about Iranian border incursions and incendiary rhetoric about Islamic revolution inside Iraq. Then, at the time of the hostage crisis between the United States and Iran, and without any diplomatic relations with the United States, Saddam attacked Iran, a country three times Iraq's territory and population, hoping to achieve a swift victory. It became the longest war of the twentieth century.

As the country was in a state of war, it was considered unpatriotic to discredit the national government. The widespread persecution of Da'wa Islamic Party members, including women, was met with silence, or justified as an act of patriotic self-defense against the "Persian enemy." Bint Al Huda al-Sadr, a leading Muslim activist, was executed with her brother, Imam Muhammad Baqir al-Sadr, following three days of torture.[60]

The communists, now expelled from government and exiled, decided to start an armed resistance based in the Kurdish area, to which they sent hundreds of their cadres, including women. Some women activists were imprisoned, others were executed. In 1981, the IWL organized its fourth conference in Beirut, challenging its previous decision to suspend activities, and issued a statement condemning the crimes of the Ba'ath regime with a list of names of forty-five female detainees.[61]

The United States decided that an Iranian victory would not serve its interests, and began supporting Iraq. In February 1982, the State Department removed Iraq from its list of states supporting international terrorism. The Ba'ath regime's links with the US administration, including Donald Rumsfeld in 1983, were justified by the Iraqi regime as strategic at a time when the country was defending itself against an enemy threatening to destabilize the region. They were also fighting the war on behalf of the Arab-Gulf states against threats from the Islamic Revolution.

Chemical weapons supplied by the West were used against the Iranians almost daily, and against the Kurdish insurgency, as well. The Massacre of Halabja took place in 1988 while the systematic destruction of Kurdish villages went on unabated. The Reagan administration decided to limit its "efforts against the Iraqi Chemical Weapons (CW) program to close monitoring because of our strict neutrality in the Gulf War, the sensitivity of sources, and the low probability of achieving desired results."[62]

"Fighting the enemy" was to the Ba'ath regime what the "War on Terror" is to the US administration. The Ba'ath, led by Saddam, who had acquired hero status, was supported by most Iraqis and had a constituency in the Arab world, creating divisions even inside Communist Parties. Dissident Iraqis, especially those sympathetic to the Islamic Da'wa party, fled to Iran and Syria, starting a series of émigré groups that later became the base of support for the US invasion and occupation of Iraq.

The social and economic position of women went through a remarkable change during the 1980s. Socially, in the aftermath of the Islamic Revolution in Iran, there was a slow rise in conservative attitudes toward women's work, but with a million men fighting the war, and the increasing cost to human life, a high proportion of jobs fell to women, including in the military.[63] Meanwhile women had to continue looking after their homes, children, and increasing numbers of disabled relatives, and to comply with the government's policy to fulfill their patriotic duty by producing more children—to compensate for those killed in the war and to face up to the enemy's higher population. Drastic measures were introduced, and, for the first time since the establishment of family-planning clinics, selling of contraceptives was prohibited.

However, in the first five years of the war, while the economy was still buoyant, the government looked after the families of war heroes in a generous way, allocating money for parents, brothers, and sisters. A widow and surviving children also received monthly pensions. But, in time, the huge financial cost of the unexpectedly protracted war forced the government to reduce its benefits.

Under a law passed in 1977, women could be commissioned as officers if they held a health-related university degree, and they could be appointed as warrant officers or noncommissioned officers (NCOs) in army medical institutes if they were qualified nurses. An increasing number of women performed in combat functions after 1981, both in the air force and in the Air Defense Command. In 1987, the People's Army (Al Jaysh ash Shaabi) was formed and women were members of it. Futuwah (Youth Vanguard) was a paramilitary organization for secondary-school students, founded in 1975. Boys and girls between the ages of fourteen and eighteen could join Futuwah and receive training in light arms, the use of grenades, and civil defense work.[64]

Therefore, many Iraqi men and women have military training. This can explain the rapid development of attacks today by the resistance, with increasing sophistication of roadside bombing and the use of the "improvised explosive device" (IED). This fact contradicts the occupation's claim that the Iraqi insurgency has been trained and led by foreign nationals or al-Qaeda.

During the war, the GFIW concentrated its efforts on promoting the regime's ideology in the media, in the Arab and Muslim world, and internationally, while continuing its work among Iraqi women, especially those in rural areas. The GFIW was also involved in the government's campaign to erase illiteracy, considered to be one of the great success stories of the Ba'ath regime.[65]

As the war dragged on, the government faced a dilemma regarding education. Despite the shortage of wartime human resources, the regime was unwilling to tap the pool of available university students, arguing that these young people were Iraq's hope for the future. As of early 1988, the government routinely exempted students from military service until graduation, a policy it adhered to rigorously.[66]

The first parliamentary elections since the 1958 revolution were held in June 1980, and the First National Assembly convened at the end of that month. As expected, Ba'ath Party candidates won 75 percent of the seats, 187 of the 250. The remaining 25 percent were won by parties allied with the Ba'ath. In the elections for the Second National Assembly in October 1984, thirty-three women were elected to the Assembly. Effective political power remained under the tight grip of the Ba'ath Party.

Ultimately the war was devastating. Both sides used brutal weapons and tactics, and the Ba'ath regime mutilated and executed its political opponents and army deserters. The families of the executed were forced to pay the price of the execution bullets in order to receive the bodies of their loved ones (as happened to my cousin Fouad al-Azzawi). This resulted in thousands of disabled young men, widows, orphans, and prisoners of war, the decline of the economy and human development, and a psychologically traumatized generation of men, women, and children.

Significant change occurred in Iraqi people's feelings and attitudes towards the Ba'ath Party and Saddam Hussein in the 1990s. By then the Ba'ath had a membership of over a million; some were genuine believers, while the rest were called "Ba'athist of signature," meaning people who had to sign the membership application forms in order to get access to certain jobs, official posts, university placement, benefits, or personal gains. Iraqis were exhausted by the eight-year Iran-Iraq War, and without being given the chance to regain their strength, they were led into another devastating war following the invasion of Kuwait. The Iraqi government accused Kuwait and the Gulf states of implementing a US agenda to weaken Iraq in the aftermath of its "victory" in the Iran-Iraq War. Furthermore, Kuwait was accused of flooding the world market with oil and producing oil illegally from Iraq's Rumaila oil field, in addition to demanding the payment of funds which were thought to be gifts.

On the eve of the invasion, Saddam Hussein summoned US ambassador April Glaspie to his office. During the meeting, Glaspie indicated that the US would not oppose his plans. Glaspie said, "I admire your extraordinary efforts to rebuild your country. I know you need funds. We understand that, and our opinion is that you should have the opportunity to rebuild your country. But we have no opinion on Arab-Arab conflicts like your border disagreement with Kuwait."[67]

In response to the invasion, the United States bombed Iraq for six weeks, destroying power stations, oil refineries, water treatment plants, and sewage plants, and contaminating the country with bombs laced with depleted uranium. The thirteen years of economic sanctions, or the "siege" as Iraqis called it, was established by UN Resolution 661 of August 6, 1990.[68] The siege touched every aspect of Iraqi life, causing death, disease, rapid economic decline, and nearly an end to any sort of human development. Unemployment increased, and people could not buy food or medicine. Health care and academic salaries declined from an average of two hundred dollars monthly before the siege, to three to ten dollars during. This was the equivalent of the price of one kilogram of meat or a few kilograms of flour. In order to survive, Iraqis had to sell every material thing of value. By the mid-nineties, half a million children died, a crime considered by many to be genocide.[69] When confronted with such statistics in 1996, Madeleine Albright, then US ambassador to the United Nations, stated that the "price was worth it" to change the Saddam regime.[70] UNICEF estimated that the first five years of sanctions against Iraq resulted in the deaths of those half a million Iraqi children under the age of five. An international public outcry condemning the injustice of the sanctions forced the UN Security Council to launch the Oil-for-Food Programme in May 1996. The program allowed Iraq to sell oil to buy its own products under UN-controlled distribution. It was well organized by the government and helped to relieve some misery, but it was not enough.

To meet the basic daily needs of the people, the government organized a monthly food ration where "everyone is entitled to the ration regardless of means and the ration and its price are uniform across the country."[71] The ration was crucial to preventing the onset of mass starvation and famine, although it met barely 35 percent of a family's nutritional needs.

Sanctions had a devastating effect on people's health, particularly on that of children and women. Consulting doctors throughout the country, particularly in the southern region, noted a remarkable increase in miscarriages, tumors (particularly breast, uterine, and blood cancer), fetal malformation and stillbirth, anemia, diabetes, and molar pregnancy.[72]

Iraqi scientists and doctors conducted considerable research into the causes of the unusual increase in cancer cases in the aftermath of the 1991 bombardment of depleted uranium (DU) by the United States and Britain, and again after its repetitive use during the "Shock and Awe" attack of 2003. Their conclusive evidence indicates that the use of DU is the cause of this new epidemic of cancer, though it has been met with complete denial by officials in both countries.[73]

The suffering of Iraqi women extended from the physical to the psychological. Fifty-seven percent of Iraqi women suffered from depression, insomnia, weight loss, and headaches due to shock caused by military bombardment, the death of their children, anxiety, and uncertainty about the future. There was an increase in the overuse of tranquilizers.[74]

The income of working women, the majority of whom were employees in the impoverished public sector, was significantly reduced after the value of the currency became less than one percent of what it was before 1991. Many professional women in cities, including those teaching and in health care, abandoned their positions since they could not afford the transportation costs, switching to work from home.

Beginning in the early 1990s, enrollment for both boys and girls fell considerably at all levels, as many were forced to leave school and enter the workforce. Moreover, lacking access to the latest texts and equipment, Iraqi schools slowly fell behind those of other countries in the region in terms of the quality of education they offered.

Nearly half of Iraqi schoolchildren had no desks in their classrooms and

Iraq's education budget fell from $500 million before the 1991 Gulf War to less than 10 percent of that in 1998 as a result of the siege.[75] Books and scientific journals were not allowed into the country; scientific research and publishing papers came almost to a halt; computer imports were restricted and related training was highly limited. The lack of educational materials forced many teachers to improvise new methods and techniques just to continue teaching children.

On December 6, 1995, I sent an A4 padded envelope to my nieces and nephews in Mosul. It contained one pencil case, three erasers, three sharpeners, six fountain pens, two markers, one glue stick, and two ballpoint pens. It was marked "gift for children." The envelope was returned, stamped: "Due to international sanctions against Iraq, we are not able to forward your packet." I was told to contact the British Department of Trade and Industry for further information.

The impact of sanctions on universities was just as drastic. Most educational materials, especially in chemistry, physics, and other sciences, were banned by the UN Sanctions Committee. Inspectors from the UN Special Commission on Iraq (UNSCOM), whose "mission was to uncover Iraqi weapons programs that continued after the 1991 Persian Gulf war,"[76] used to inspect universities laboratories and libraries to confiscate chemistry books and burn them. Students who were determined to carry on with their studies were also faced with the constant threat of US bombings and renewed American military aggression.[77]

In 1993, *Al Hamla al imaniya*, "The Faith Campaign," was officially initiated by Saddam Hussein, and was widely understood by Iraqis as a sign of the regime attempting to deal with the harsh reality of the sanctions and to follow the trend in Iraq, the region as a whole, and indeed in the United States, to turn toward faith-based politics. Under the sanctions, people were looking for security in traditions. There were more strategic and ideological reasons for the regime's gradual shedding of its extreme secular views since the end of the war with Iran in 1988, and the waning of that particular Islamic threat. The Iraqi pan-Arab movement was opening up to the Islamists, and Saddam Hussein added in his own handwriting the words *Allah Akbar* ("God is the greatest") to the Iraqi flag, as a symbolic response to adversaries like Iran and Saudi Arabia whose flags also have Islamic writings. It helped to garner the material and moral support of the Muslims of the world during the war of 1991 and the sanction years.[78]

The regime established a university for Islamic Sciences, with regional branches for the training of Muslim clerics. Another special college was assigned to the Ba'ath Party itself so that all the high government officials could be trained. At the mass level, the study of the Qur'an became compulsory in all the schools. A radio station was assigned to sixteen hours of Qur'an reciting, and the proportion allotted to religion in all the media and newspapers was increased. The government took over the informal courses in mosques that teach the Qur'an and its interpretations, built hundreds of new mosques in partnership with philanthropists offering endowments, and organized competitions for the rote learning of the Qur'an. All of these were open to both sexes. The inclusion of courses for Arabic language, poetry, and diction was popular for young girls as much as boys, even in families that had no particular interest in the faith itself.

There was an obvious security advantage for the regime in this use of religion, as the mosques reverted to their original functions as the town hall and public gathering places, made especially useful after the collapse of the state. The regime was trying to weaken the hold of Shi'a and Sunni religious schools by reclaiming Islam and its public space, the mosque, that had been used by religious and nonreligious opposition groups, promoting some state-controlled modern version of both, and accepting the shari'a edicts common to both. Horse racing, the only traditionally accepted form of gambling in Iraq, was banned, and so was the sale of alcohol in public. Women were included in all this state-religious activity, but with time, the mandatory hijab, which was violently opposed by the regime during the 1980, gradually spread, although without a specific official endorsement.

The Ba'ath regime had tried to ease the economical burden on the Iraqi people through state and individual initiatives. It had successes in publicly supported efforts to rebuild the infrastructure. Dedicated Iraqi engineers restored the electricity grid and rebuilt the destroyed bridges in a few months, a matter of pride for Iraqis to this day.

After the destruction of the nuclear program, scientists were moved to various state departments to help restore the damaged public facilities. And contrary to what was publicized in the media, the regime increased expenditure in the health sector after 1996, and in 1997 signed supply and logistics contracts worth $2.1 billion. The Ministry of Islamic Affairs had set up a fund for alms to provide for needy individuals and families. Social solidarity funds had also been set up in many ministries and departments through informal and spontaneous initiatives. The family welfare salary, which was issued in accordance with Law Number 126 of 1980, was the most important and sustainable regulation to date. The GFIW tried to change its role from that of a state propaganda tool directed toward women to that of a partially independent organization working with women. Some steps were taken with help from the United Nations Development Programme (UNDP) and United Nations Development Fund for Women (UNIFEM).

A relatively large-scale social-solidarity program was launched to help poor women and their families with the provision of clothes, food baskets, and medical treatment for children with chronic diseases. Assistance had been allocated to widows and divorcées supporting their families, as well as to malnourished children. Under agreement with the UNDP, the Ministry of Labor and Social Affairs launched a small-loan program in 1996 as an attempt to reduce women's poverty and began a pilot program in two main cities, covering thirty projects that included poultry farms, foodstuff processing, ceramics, printing, football, industry, sewing, and embroidery. A credit fund for women who wanted to set up small household projects and those intending to pursue their academic education was also established, with 50 percent of the fund's capital coming from the Federation and the remaining 50 percent from individual women.[79]

A National Strategy for Advancing the Status of Iraqi Women was planned, and independent publications on cultural and women's issues were published, such as *Shahrazad* magazine in 2000, *Al Jandar* (*Gender*) newspaper in 2001, *Bulletin* in 2001 (from the Women's Research Unit at Baghdad University), and *Afaq* (Horizon) literary magazine in 2002. In order to revitalize its work among professional women and intellectuals, the GFIW also established two new branches: Al Mihaniyat (Professional Women) and the Cultural Forum for Women. The latter enjoyed some unusual freedom in organizing cultural events, poetry readings, exhibitions, and study groups.[80]

These efforts, however, were seen by the majority of Iraqi women as being too little too late. There was, of course, a slight change in policy after the signing of the UN Memorandum of Understanding in 1996, and following the shrinking of state funds and willingness to elevate the economic burden on women under sanctions.

In his 2000 study evaluating the Federation's activities, Dr. Nabil al-Nawab highlighted the difficulty of considering the GFIW a civil-society organization. This organization of over a million members, with offices in all provinces and branches in most districts, and involving diverse roles with the state, was the equivalent of a ministry for women's affairs. It might well have been considered akin to Soviet-style unions and mass organizations, with its mixture of social welfare functions, mobilization ability, and sounding boards on social policies. Al-Nawab also highlighted its limited resources due to sanctions, and the need for the GFIW to develop its organizational structure, reinforce decentralization, and better interact and make contact with its beneficiaries.

This would have been a difficult task to achieve, as the GFIW remained in Iraqi eyes a propaganda arm of an oppressive regime; its changes were perceived as cosmetic. The GFIW, like the US-funded women's organizations under occupation, had met the suffering of Iraqi women with silence, justifying the Ba'ath policies against political opponents even when the party was issuing disastrous decrees against women's basic human rights, such as prohibiting women to travel abroad on their own unless accompanied by a brother or a father, or issuing its 1990 presidential decree granting immunity to men who committed honor crimes, a revival of a receding tribal practice which gives male family members the right to murder female family members who are perceived to have brought dishonor upon the family by engaging in (or suspected of being engaged in) an illicit sexual relationship.

In the 1990s, the brutality against uprisings in the south and north, the two "no-fly zones" (imposed by the United States, Britain, and France without authorization by the UN, an intervention justified as a humanitarian effort to protect Shi'a Muslims in the south and Kurds in the north), and the lack of cash for material improvements, left the regime almost naked in front of its people. Supporters were thin on the ground. Furthermore, the harshness of the sanctions was associated in people's minds with the presence of the Ba'ath regime. Few Iraqis remained willing to defend it.

Poverty, hunger, and intellectual stagnation forced many people to flee the country, among them writers, artists, poets, and academics. The irony is that the mass exodus in the 1990s, with the exception of the people who were involved in the southern uprising, came about for economic reasons and at a time when the regime's oppressive grip was weakening. Economic deprivation and corruption resulted in deterioration in education, health, and public services. As in the 1970s, the economy and the utilization of revenue proved once again the major factor in determining the people's loyalty to or rejection of the Ba'ath regime.

II Invading Iraq

In the United States and Britain, little was heard about the plight of Iraqi women under Saddam Hussein's regime until the build-up to war was in its final stages. The suffering of the Iraqi people caused by oppression, sanctions, and US–UK aerial bombardments was generally ignored, except by a few humanitarian and international organizations and independent journalists.

It was not until October 2002 that the US administration adopted the issue of Iraqi women and called for their liberation. Several US-funded Iraqi women's organizations were established immediately before and after the invasion. In some cases, they were attached to existing opposition groups and parties; in others, they were independent, calling themselves nongovernmental organizations (NGOs). These NGOs played a significant role in mobilizing public and political support for the war on Iraq. After the war, they have continued to play an important role in the media—more in the United States than in Iraq—as advocates for US policy in Iraq.

In reality, the United States and its colonial feminists have been irrelevant for the majority of Iraqi women, and have impeded the much-needed work by genuine independent women's organizations.[1] The rhetoric of women's empowerment, and the training of a handful of Iraqi women leaders on the principles and practices of democracy at conferences organized outside Iraq, have nothing to do with the daily lives of women who live in dire poverty, have been displaced from their homes, or are living in tents, lacking basic sanitation and supplies. Female illiteracy in Iraq is at the highest level since the 1930s, and privatization threatens free public services. In the mayhem of daily bloodshed, they suffer abuse of their rights, both from the government and from increasing localized gender-based violence. Unemployment has fueled prostitution, back-street abortions, "honor killings," and domestic violence. The puppet regime's colonial feminists are either cynical or blind to the sharp contrasts between their rhetoric and reality. In the spirit of the US administration's axiom,

"No one's saying it's going to be an easy transition,"[2] the colonial feminists have justified the massive death toll as an unavoidable necessity.

In order to understand the nature of the activities and projects of these women's organizations inside and outside Iraq, we need to examine first the sources of funding, and second, the changes in US policy toward NGOs after September 11, 2001.[3]

After Bush issued the dictum, "You are either with us or against us," the role of NGOs was transformed to meet the requirements of the "War on Terror." Former secretary of state Colin Powell outlined the new vision when, addressing NGOs in 2001, he argued, "Just as surely as our diplomats and military, American NGOs are out there serving and sacrificing on the frontlines of freedom. NGOs are such a force multiplier for us, such an important part of our combat team."[4] Andrew Natsios, the administrator for the US Agency for International Development (USAID), which was coordinating the rebuilding of Iraq, bluntly spelled out the same vision. He told international humanitarian leaders that "NGOs and contractors are an arm of the US government," and that in order to serve Washington's political and military objectives, aid agencies "should identify themselves as recipients of US funding."[5] Justifying the action, he stated, "The work we do is now perceived to affect the national survival of the US." Knowing that nearly all US NGOs receive over half of their funding from government sources, Natsios's harsh language was not taken lightly.[6]

The most prominent US-funded NGOs that went to work inside Iraq immediately after the declaration of "mission accomplished" were Women for a Free Iraq (WFFI), the Women's Alliance for a Democratic Iraq (WAFDI), the Iraq Foundation, and the American Islamic Congress (AIC).[7] Their funding came primarily from the US State Department; USAID; the International Republican Institute (IRI); the National Democratic Institute (NDI), whose chair is Madeleine Albright; and the Independent Women's Forum (IWF).

Inside Iraq, the budget allocated to women's NGOs amounted to several million US dollars. According to Paul Bremer, on June 30, 2004, on the eve of handing over sovereignty to Iyad Allawi's[8] interim government, Bremer had "allocated almost $750 million from the American and Iraqi budgets. Much of the program was meant to build the institutions and organizations that formed what we westerners call civil society."[9] Judy Van Rest explained to Allawi that "we are establishing these institutions all over Iraq . . . our provincial offices [have] midwifed the birth of dozens of human rights centers, nongovernmental organizations, legal associations, even PTAs. We had funds to set up women's centers in all eighteen provinces, nine in Baghdad alone."[10] In fact, this money was mainly spent on organizing conferences, mostly outside Iraq, and training selected women to be leaders on "democracy." According to a fact sheet issued by the US State Department's Office of the Senior Coordinator for International Women's Issues on June 22, 2005, "The United States allocated nearly half a billion dollars to support democracy-building programs in Iraq—including projects that specifically help women with democratic organization and advocacy."[11]

Tracing the history of how some of these organizations came to be established will shed light on their role as civil-society organizations intended to be the "soft occupiers" in the aftermath of liberation. On October 4, 2002, at a highly publicized official event called "The Unheard Voices of Iraqi Women," held at the National Press Club in Washington DC, the audience was invited to listen to accounts of Saddam's persecution of women as told by "seven Iraqi women of different regional, ethnic and religious backgrounds."[12] The event was sponsored by the International Alliance for Justice (IAJ), which has Congressional funding, and was attended by Safia Taleb al-Suhail, the IAJ advocacy director for the Middle East and Islamic world. The panel also included Zakia Ismail Hakki, a lawyer and former president of the Kurdish Women's Foundation, and Katrin Michael, a member of the Iraqi opposition in Washington, who lived through chemical attacks unleashed by Saddam Hussein on Iraq's Kurdish population in June 1987.

Katrin Michael, who joined the Iraqi Women's League[13] as a teenager and had lived in the United States since 1997, explained in an interview on December 12, 2002, only five months before the invasion, how the US administration had ignored Iraqi women's rights. Her goal was "to make the women of Iraq as visible to the American public as the women of Afghanistan were a year ago, when the Bush administration criticized the Taliban for its repressive attitude toward the country's women and girls."[14] More importantly, she wanted to make the administration take note of the presence of women within the opposition. The leading roles on the stage of war were already approved. Female players were allocated secondary parts as needed. This division of labor would reflect badly on colonial feminists once "the mission was accomplished" inside Iraq, when dividing the spoils of war reached its height among sectarian and ethnic parties.

Michael complained about the small role allotted to women despite the increase in their political activities and the high percentage they represented in the population. "Over the last four months, the Iraqi opposition groups have been very active in Washington, having many meetings with the State Department. But where are the women in the opposition?"[15]

Similar moves were made in London. Following Washington's last minute realization that it could make use of the suffering of Iraqi women to build up public support for the war, Tony Blair had his own meeting with Iraqi women in Downing Street. In November 2002, one month after "The Unheard Voices of Iraqi Women" event in Washington, the British prime minister met a group of seven Iraqi women in London, two of whom wept as they told him their stories.[16] There is no doubt that many of the Iraqi women's stories were true, and that some of the women who spoke out at staged events in the prewar period hoped naively that their stories of life under Saddam would help in getting rid of Saddam's regime and build a better future for all Iraqis.

Others, however, were not that naive. They were, as their political affiliation indicates, highly aware of the significant role they were to play in mobilizing public and political support for the war on their country. While telling their "untold stories," they chose "to present the human rights case for intervention in Iraq,"[17] when the case for war was thin. Thus, they chose to be the female face of the invasion, and came to be seen by most Iraqis as colonial feminists.[18]

In the period leading up to the invasion, when millions of people around the world were demonstrating against a preemptive war, none of them defending Saddam's regime or dismissing his crimes, but concerned about the safety of the Iraqi people, colonial feminists spared little concern for their sisters who would suffer. The war has been, in the final analysis, a war on Iraqi women.

A month before the invasion, in February 2003,[19] the Foundation for the Defense of Democracies (FDD)[20] brought together fifty Iraqi women (most of them US citizens) to establish Women for a Free Iraq (WFFI), a sister organization of the IAJ. It was also funded by the Committee for the Liberation of Iraq (CLI). The Bush administration rapidly embraced the new organization. WFFI was baptized at a meeting attended by Vice President Dick Cheney, National Security Advisor Condoleezza Rice, Deputy Secretary of Defense Paul Wolfowitz, Under Secretary of State for Global Affairs Paula Dobriansky, and Ambassador at Large for a Free Iraq Zalmay Khalilzad. At the meeting, the Iraqi women shared their experiences under Saddam's reign of terror.[21]

On the same day, March 6, 2003, WFFI was launched publicly at the Foreign Press Center in Washington, DC, by Paula Dobriansky. The launch was attended by prominent members of WFFI: Tanya Gilly, Director of Democracy Programs, at the FDD; Zainab al-Suwaij; Maha Alattar; and Esra Naama, who had been received earlier in the day by White House officials. Maha Alattar was raised in Baghdad and left for the United States at the age of thirteen. She is president of the Iraqi Forum for Democracy, a nonprofit organization promoting democracy in Iraq. She currently resides in North Carolina. Esra Naama left Iraq after the Gulf War. She was ten years old. After the invasion, she was employed in December 2003 by Eileen Padberg, who was asked by the San Diego consulting firm Katz & Associates to help arrange a "woman small business component" of a contract to manage a $4.4 billion water-reconstruction contract in Iraq.[22] Tanya Gilly read the WFFI statement, which made no mention of the administration's systematic silence over many decades on the plight of the Iraqi people, its support for Saddam Hussein's regime, especially during the Iran-Iraq War, and the US- and UK-backed economic sanctions against the Iraqi people. Instead, she simply stated, "We are women who fled from Iraq to escape persecution by Saddam Hussein's regime. We have come together to speak up about the suffering of the Iraqi people under his regime and their yearning to be liberated."

The statement of WFFI went on to praise the US administration. It offered support "to President Bush for his principled leadership," and applauded "the determination of the American government to disarm Saddam, and its commitment to help liberate the people of Iraq." The WFFI statement was to become the blueprint for Iraqi women "leaders" whenever they visited the United States after the invasion.

The role of WFFI was to support the Bush administration's line on the war on Iraq, and to make Saddam Hussein appear such a threat to the people of the United States that immediate action needed to be taken against him. They warned that "the cost of inaction and appeasement would be very high for the people of America and Iraq, alike; and even the Middle East. . . . We know from personal experience that Saddam cannot be contained and will always be a danger to the world."[23]

The FDD, like the US administration, had not shown any interest in the suffering of Iraqi women before the build-up to the invasion. Their interest in the plight of Iraqi women was conveniently introduced for reasons best explained by them: "When President George W. Bush was considering intervention in Iraq, the FDD recognized that important voices were missing from the debate—those of Iraqis with personal experience of Saddam Hussein's oppression, brutality and genocide. The FDD brought together a group of Iraqi women who could help Americans understand what had been taking place in Iraq—and what was at stake there."[24]

On March 20, 2003, the United States launched its first series of air strikes on Baghdad. Iraqi people had to experience the "Shock and Awe" of US airpower and to live the day-to-day tragedy of war and death again. Iraqi women, who had already suffered tremendously under thirteen years of sanctions and war, were in a frenzy as they struggled for their own and their families' survival. In the weeks preceding the first bombardments, they dug wells in their backyards or gardens, queued to get their food rations for the next six months, stored as much imperishable food and powdered milk for babies as they could get, and stockpiled gas cylinders and gasoline, despite the risks involved. Some families, particularly in Baghdad, decided to leave their homes in the main cities and sought refuge with friends and relatives in towns and villages in the country. With fears of medical shortages and concerns about being able to reach hospitals in time, pregnant women queued to have cesarean births. Luma, my twenty-four-year-old niece, was one of hundreds of these women. She wasn't due for another month.

It is ironic that, on the same day as the air strikes, the Office of International Women's Issues at the State Department produced a leaflet entitled "Iraqi Women Under Saddam's Regime: A Population Silenced," which demonstrated US support for Iraqi women and further demonized Saddam's regime. While Baghdad was being shaken to its foundations by B52 bombings, and while US-led troops were using thousands of tons of DU explosives and cluster bombs against the population, destroying much of the Iraqi civilian infrastructure that had been rebuilt after the 1991 war, members of WFFI made more than two hundred media appearances, including an interview with Barbara Walters, to "offer their support to President Bush for his principled leadership."[25] With the FDD's help, they visited the White House twice for meetings and photo opportunities with the president, the vice president, and the national security advisor. While Iraqi women were mourning the deaths of their loved ones and the destruction of their country, WFFI women were instrumental in rallying support for the "liberation of Iraq." As one of them, Esra Naama, put it to the press: "We want to thank President Bush and the troops that are there in the desert. Thank you for helping my people and for going to liberate my country."[26]

WFFI spawned other organizations as well.[27] Several US-funded Iraqi women's groups were established either immediately before or after the invasion. On April 21, a few days after Bush declared his "mission accomplished," nineteen members of WFFI attended a meeting to form the Women's Alliance for a Democratic Iraq (WAFDI), in order to be eligible for international aid. WAFDI is described as "an international non-partisan and not-for-profit women's rights organization, dedicated to a free and democratic Iraq with full and equal individual rights for women." Some WAFDI members moved with the troops inside Iraq to develop "projects to advance women's participation in rebuilding Iraqi civil society."[28]

Another organization closely linked to WFFI and the FDD is the American Islamic Congress (AIC). It was set up after September 11, 2001, by an Iraqi-American woman named Zainab al-Suwaij, herself a founding member of WFFI. Al-Suwaij moved to Iraq with US forces to be actively engaged in reconstruction projects in Iraq, and claimed to represent Iraqi women, who have in the past played a very small role in Iraqi politics.

After "liberation," the FDD moved in again to lead the way in "building Iraqi civil society." It set up an umbrella organization for US-funded Iraqi NGOs, called the Iraq-America Freedom Alliance (IAFA), which describes itself as "a non-partisan group of American and Iraqi organizations and individuals that work to inform the public about the positive changes occurring in Iraq. Thanks to the U.S. military and other courageous Americans, we are winning the war on terror and promoting a free Iraq." Its members include WFFI, WAFDI, the American Islamic Congress, and the Iraq Foundation, which was established in 1991 by Kanaan Makia and Rend al-Rahim Francke. Kanaan Makia is a member of the board of directors of AIC, and a leading figure in the National Congress Party under Ahmed Chalabi. He is famous for his prediction to President Bush, on the eve of the invasion, that "Iraqis will receive the Americans with sweets and flowers." Rend al-Rahim Francke is the executive director of the Iraq Foundation, which changed its name to the Iraq Memory Foundation.

Although these and other organizations based in Britain are registered under a variety of names and claim varying objectives and programs, they have, in fact, been established and run by the same handful of Iraqi women.[29]

■ ■ ■

After the invasion, the US administration used colonial feminists and their NGOs when it needed to justify its policies and the continued military occupation, and to cover up the chaos created by the war and its failures in the fight against terrorism and Islamist fundamentalism.

The IAFA and the FDD both played a role in the 2004 US presidential election campaign. They were exceptionally active during the summer and fall of 2004, organizing speaking tours for a dozen Iraqi "women leaders" from inside Iraq, the highlight of which was a photo op with George Bush.[30] They shared their stories of oppression under Saddam Hussein's regime and expressed their gratitude for their liberation. They spoke to audiences and local media in twenty cities across the United States, visited military bases to thank US soldiers for their sacrifices in Iraq, and painted a rosy picture of Bush's mission in Iraq. They appeared in print and broadcast media more than five hundred times.[31]

WAFDI worked closely with Deputy Secretary of Defense Paul Wolfowitz "to create a bi-partisan agenda that would showcase the political process from the local level up to the White House."[32] In his remarks to a delegation of Iraqi women leaders who were in the United States for practical training in the workings of democracy, he urged the women to thank the soldiers themselves who participated in their liberation. After the reelection of President Bush, the FDD continued to support and finance WFFI, WAFDI, and others, organizing their efforts when needed in the service of US policy. The Foundation, for example, arranged for selected Iraqi women "to speak at the White House and to members of Congress, organized letter-writing campaigns to Ambassador Bremer and the Iraqi Governing Council and built coalitions on behalf of Iraqi women that included liberal and conservative American women's groups."[33] Their letters to US officials included such expressions as "we must all continue to fight evil," and are written under the heading, "The mission of the mothers and the daughters of the new Iraq."[34]

The FDD was not the only supplier of funds to these organizations. They were fed from other sources. The FDD was awarded a grant under the State Department's Iraqi Women's Education Initiative to run a "Women's Leadership Program." The Iraqi Women's Educational Institute (IWEI) worked in partnership with the AIC and the IWF. When US Under Secretary of State for Global Affairs Paula Dobriansky announced the $10 million grant, she said, "We will give Iraqi women the tools. We will provide the information and experience they need to run for office, and lobby for fair treatment in Iraq's emerging institutions." The fact that the money would go mainly to organizations with strong links to the US administration, such as the Independent Women's Forum (IWF) founded by Dick Cheney's wife, Lynne Cheney, was not mentioned, nor was it mentioned that Dobriansky herself had also served on the IWF's board of advisers.[35]

These training conferences continued in tandem with the US-driven political process in Iraq, the handing over of sovereignty, the elections, and the drafting of the constitution, for example. In April 2005, IWEI hosted a conference of Iraqi women leaders in Jordan. It was sponsored by the IWF, the AIC, and the FDD, and was funded by the IRI and NDI, who are said to have received $80 million for the Iraqi elections.

Within Iraqi society, the role of women's NGOs has been confined to supporting the political process and campaigning to preserve women's rights in Iraq's new constitution. On August 4, 2005, representatives of two women's groups were in Washington, DC, to rally support for their cause. Zainab al-Suwaij, executive director of the AIC, and Basma Fakri, of WAFDI, appeared at a "newsmaker" event at the National Press Club, to represent other newly established Iraq-based organizations: the More Than One Source campaign[36] and the Iraqi Women's Network (Amal). Leaders of the campaign in Iraq include Rend al-Rahim Francke and Safia Taleb al-Suhail.[37] Tanya Gilly from FDD argued for the need to seek foreign support for the Iraqi women's cause.

In 2005, FDD launched the Iraq Democracy Information Center, a Web-based guide to educational materials on democracy, distributed by its partner, the AIC, in Iraq. It also offered its support to Friends of Democracy (FOD), which was established in October 2004 by Spirit of America, a nonprofit mainly targeting women and students. FOD, an American NGO, aims "to provide support to those on the frontlines: American military and civilian personnel and people who call to Americans for help in their struggle for freedom."[38] Needless to say, the Spirit of America projects in Iraq are a reflection of US foreign policy. They see the occupation, the US military presence, and its continuous crimes against the Iraqi population as the way to establish democracy.

Look at the way Spirit of America dealt with the Coalition Provisional Authority's weakness in the war of ideas, images, and public relations, as the organization undertook the project to upgrade seven defunct Iraqi-owned television stations in the western Anbar province in the second year of occupation:

> If Jim Hake (a successful technology entrepreneur who has been working with the Marine Corps) can raise $100,000, his Spirit of America will buy the equipment in the U.S., ship it to the Marines in Iraq and get Iraqi-run TV on the air before the June 30 handover.
>
> If the Marines can get these moribund stations back on the air, the coverage area would include Fallujah and Ramadi. The VHF/UHF stations are owned as cooperatives by TV-competent Iraqis already vetted by the Army.
>
> Some broadcast *Al-Jazeera* for lack of other content. In return for the upgrades, the Iraqi operators would be asked two things: criticism is fine, but don't run anti-coalition propaganda; and let the Marines buy air time to broadcast public-service announcements, such as the reopening of schools or clinics—or indeed, pending military operations.[39]

In Iraq, Spirit of America promotes the essence of vetted democracy—that is, democracy without citizenship—thereby flooding the public with information promoting itself and marginalizing dissent.

But these US-UK government-sponsored NGOs have underestimated the nationalist sentiments of Iraqi people and their deep-rooted feelings against occupation. It has become obvious to Iraqis that these NGOs are nothing but subcontractors acting on behalf of the occupation forces to infiltrate and undermine a legitimate Iraqi society and its grassroots organizations. Colonial feminists have confused the need to get rid of a tyrannical regime with the imposition of a new colonial order.[40] By lining up women behind nominally progressive goals, the occupation diverts attention away from the main issue of independence, and at the same time hinders the growth of indigenous women's organizations aiming to be part of the process of establishing democracy.

■ ■ ■

While human rights abuses against Iraqis are ignored by the United States and its client government, there has been no shortage of initiatives to "enlighten" Iraqi women about their role in building democracy under occupation. In one, the Department for International Development and the British Foreign Office declared "the need, urgently, for a women's tent meeting in Baghdad with a declaration in compliance with 1325."[41] Patricia Hewitt, the British Minister for Women and Equality, tried to establish a high council for Iraqi women. On March 6, 2003, she said, "If we do fight in Iraq, it will be to uphold international law and to get rid of weapons of mass destruction, but the defeat of Saddam will also be the liberation of the women of Iraq." Condoleezza Rice opened a center for women's human rights in Diwanya. In her opening speech—delivered via satellite—she assured Iraqi women that "we are with you in spirit." It was attended by commanders and soldiers of the occupying forces, but by very few Iraqi women. At the same time, in Diwanya itself, local farmers (many of them women) were unable to start the winter sowing season because of unexploded cluster bombs on their land.

Meanwhile, many colonial feminists were allocated positions as MPs in the three consequent Iraqi governments or later. How relevant is this development? Political participation, though higher than in any other Arab country due to the quota system, remains, as under Saddam's regime, nominal. There were two female members out of the twenty-five in the Iraqi Governing Council,[42] which set the sectarian, ethnic, and gender blueprint for the interim government that followed: the "elected" government, the membership of the parliament, and the drafting of the constitution. The presidency of Iraq, which rotated monthly among nine members of the council, were of course all men.[43]

On June 30, 2004, Paul Bremer handed over sovereignty to Allawi's interim government, which included six women among the thirty ministers named. Following a timetable designed and imposed by Bremer, it was replaced in May 2005 by the Iraqi Interim Government, which was then replaced on May 20, 2006, by the first permanent government. There are four women in the thirty-seven-member cabinet.[44] A Ministry for Women's Affairs was established for the first time. In all three governments women, were allocated to service ministries.

How effective are women in high official positions? The image of Safia Taleb al-Suhail—a founding member of WFFI, an adviser to the Iraqi Ministry on Foreign Affairs, and the appointed Iraqi ambassador to Egypt—hugging Mrs. Janet Norwood, whose son was killed in Iraq, could be used as an example to illustrate the gap between the media's use of images of women and the reality, between Iraqi women and the colonial feminists claiming to speak on our behalf. On February 2, 2005, Safia Taleb al-Suhail was invited to attend Bush's State of the Union address, the careful staging of which was designed to promote a president whose Iraqi policy was becoming increasingly unpopular at home. The *Washington Times* reported: "The powerful moment, a snapshot of the sacrifices Americans have made to free Iraq from dictator Saddam Hussein, came near the end of the president's address, when Safia Taleb al-Suhail, turned and reached up to Mrs. Norwood. The two embraced as the applause grew to a crescendo. The president, visibly moved, looked up from the podium as the seconds stretched to a full minute—the longest applause of the evening. Mrs. Norwood's son was killed Nov. 13 by sniper fire during the assault on the terrorist stronghold of Fallujah, Iraq."[45]

The reality of what happened in Fallujah and how it affected Iraqi women was very different. On November 8, 2004, after more than two months of aerial attacks, the United States began its second major assault on Fallujah, bringing about widespread devastation and killing hundreds of civilians. British forces supported the attack with hundreds of troops redeployed to form part of a "ring of steel" around the city.

The scale of the attack and its effect on civilians was unprecedented in the bloody history of the invasion and occupation.[46] Much of Fallujah was destroyed, and hundreds of thousands of residents became refugees. On November 7, 2005, Italian satellite television broadcast a film with evidence that the United States had used white phosphorus weapons. The program, *Fallujah: The Concealed Massacre*, by RAI News correspondent Sigfrido Ranucci, carried interviews with US military personal. One interviewee, a former American soldier who fought at Fallujah, says, "I heard the order to pay attention because they were going to use white phosphorus on Fallujah. In military jargon it's known as Willy Pete. . . . Phosphorus burns bodies, in fact it melts the flesh all the way down to the bone. . . . I saw the burned bodies of women and children. Phosphorus explodes and forms a cloud. Anyone within a radius of 150 meters is done for."[47]

North American reporter Dahr Jamail, of the Inter Press Service, interviewed a doctor who had filmed the testimony of a teenage girl: "One story is of a young girl who is 16 years old, he says of one of the testimonies he videotaped recently. She stayed for three days with the bodies of her family who were killed in their home. When the soldiers entered she was in her home with her father, mother, 12-year-old brother and two sisters. She watched the soldiers enter and shoot her mother and father directly, without saying anything."

The girl managed to hide behind the refrigerator with her brother and witnessed the war crimes firsthand. "They beat her two sisters, and then shot them in the head," the doctor said. After this her brother was enraged and ran at the soldiers while shouting at them, so they shot him dead. "She continued hiding after the soldiers left and stayed with her sisters because they were bleeding, but still alive. She was too afraid to call for help because she feared the soldiers would come back and kill her as well. She stayed for three days, with no water and no food. Eventually one of the American snipers saw her and took her to the hospital."

Jamail says that the doctor told him of another story that he had documented, of a mother who was in her home during the siege. "On the fifth day of the siege her home was bombed, and the roof fell on her son, cutting his legs off. For hours she couldn't go outside because they announced that anyone going in the street would be shot. So all she could do was wrap his legs and watch him die before her eyes."[48]

A year after the attack, the *New York Times* described Fallujah as "virtually a police state," with random checkpoints and frequent street patrols by marines and Iraqi soldiers. *Sunday Times* reporter Hala Jaber found it "impossible not to be shocked by the devastation, with "[f]ields of rubble stretch[ing] for as far as the eye can see." In July 2005, the rubble was still there and an estimated fifty thousand people had yet to return to the city.

More than six hundred Iraqis have been killed in Fallujah since marines began the siege, most of them women, children, and the elderly. Bodies were being buried in two soccer fields, one of which was visited by an Associated Press reporter. It was filled with row after row of graves.[49] Around Fallujah, camps have been erected to receive displaced women and children. Men aged fifteen to fifty were not allowed to leave the city, so 150,000 wait in anguish for news of fathers, husbands, and sons. The execution-style killing of a wounded Iraqi inside a mosque by a US marine, captured by NBC television, was one of many, according to an eyewitness interviewed by al-Jazeera television.[50]

Since Fallujah, the United States has continued to attack other towns and cities in Iraq, including Ramadi, Hit, Baghdad, Haditha, Qa'im, Karbala, Tal Afar, and Samarra. During the period from October 1, 2005, to February 6, 2006, US warplanes under the control of US Central Command attacked at least twenty-two Iraqi cities—twice the number struck during the same five-month period one year earlier.[51] Yet all members of the successive governments in the Green Zone, including the female cabinet ministers, have greeted the suffering of Iraqi civilians, whose cities are showered with napalm, white phosphorus, and cluster bombs, with rhetoric about training for democracy.

Several documents released on March 7, 2005, by the American Civil Liberties Union (ACLU) show thirteen cases of rape and abuse of female detainees. The documents reveal that no action was taken against any soldier or civilian official as a result. The documents provide further evidence that US troops have destroyed evidence of abuse and torture in order to avoid a repetition of the Abu Ghraib prison abuse scandal.

One of the major shortcomings of women in office is their failure to represent the real-life concerns of Iraqi women. Because of their commitment to party politics and the US political agenda in Iraq, they have been highly selective in their response to the plight of Iraqi women. This was manifested visibly during the political row over the interim Governing Council's attempt to adopt Islamic shari'a through Resolution 137, and in drafting the constitution. The Council's response was also influenced by the fact that most of the female ministers and the few in high official positions have been the directors of US-funded women's organizations, which played a vital role in mobilizing public opinion to launch the war on Iraq in the first place.

In August 2005, a group of Iraqi women who backed the US-UK invasion met the American ambassador Zalmay Khalilzad, in an effort to pressure the politicians drawing up Iraq's constitution not to limit women's rights. Western feminist groups and some Iraqi women activists feared that Islamic law, if enshrined as a main source of legislation, would be used to restrict their rights, particularly in relation to marriage, divorce, and inheritance. The United States claims to share this concern, but Iraqi women generally do not, since at this point the battle over the constitution is regarded by most survival-seeking Iraqi women as irrelevant.

This attitude was reinforced when the United States presented the interim government of Iyad Allawi with a draft constitution that was put together by a New York University assistant professor named Noah Feldman. Upon learning about this appointment, the late Edward Said wrote:

> It was recently announced in the U.S. press that a 32-year-old assistant professor of law, Noah Feldman, at New York University, would be responsible for producing a new Iraqi constitution. It was mentioned in all the media accounts of this major appointment that Feldman was an extraordinarily brilliant expert in Islamic law, had studied Arabic since he was 15, and grew up as an Orthodox Jew. But he has never practiced law in the Arab world, never been to Iraq, and seems to have no real practical background in the problems of post-war Iraq. What an open-faced snub not only to Iraq itself, but also to the legions of Arab and Muslim legal minds who could have done a perfectly acceptable job in the service of Iraq's future. But no, America wants it done by a fresh young fellow, so as to be able to say, "we have given Iraq its new democracy."[52]

Here are some facts to keep in mind: Only nine of the seventy-one members of the constitutional committee were women, a choice of the committee members, which reflected the sectarian ethnic divide that characterized the interim government. The constitution had been voted upon in a war zone, in a country on the verge of civil war. The process of writing it was designed not to represent the Iraqi people's needs but to comply with an imposed timetable aimed at legitimizing the occupation. The United States mounted considerable pressure on Iraqis to meet the August 15, 2005, deadline. From the US administration's point of view, any delay would mark a setback to US efforts to maintain political momentum to combat the insurgency.

Secretary of State Condoleezza Rice made a surprise visit to Iraq, encouraging Iraq's fledgling government to cope with the insurgency and to swiftly draft a new, inclusive constitution. In blunt words, US Secretary of Defense Donald Rumsfeld urged Iraqis to complete their new constitution on time when he arrived in Baghdad on one of his unannounced visits. "Now's the time to get on with it," he said, calling for the committee writing it to meet its August 15 deadline. Tony Blair and Jack Straw followed in his footsteps. The constitution proved to be a dividing rather than a unifying document, to the extent that its American author had to advise, "The less the constitution says about controversial issues, the greater the likelihood that it will be ratified."[53]

What value has a constitution, if not applied? Under Saddam Hussein, Iraq had a constitution described widely in the Arab world as progressive and secular. It was based on the Provisional Constitution of July 16, 1970, which had been modified several times. It proclaimed Iraq to be "a sovereign people's democratic republic." Islam was declared to be the state religion, but freedom of religion and of religious practices was guaranteed. Iraq was formed of two principal nationalities, Arab and Kurd. A March 1974 amendment to the Constitution provided autonomy for the Kurds in the region where they constituted a majority of the population. In this autonomous region, both Arabic and Kurdish were designated as official languages for administrative and educational purposes. The Constitution also prescribed, however, that the "national rights" of the Kurds, as well as the "legitimate rights" of all minorities, were to be exercised only within the framework of Iraqi unity, and the document stipulated that no part of Iraq could be relinquished.

Articles 19 through 36 of the Constitution spelled out the fundamental rights and duties in detail. The right to fair trial through due process, the inviolability of person and of residence, the privacy of correspondence, and the freedom to travel were guaranteed to all citizens. The Constitution also assured citizens of their right to religious freedom; to the freedom of speech, of publication, and of assembly; and to the freedom to form political parties, trade unions, and professional societies. The Constitution directed the state to eliminate illiteracy and to ensure the right of citizens to free education, from elementary school through to the university level. The Constitution also required the state to provide every citizen with employment and with free medical care. Article 25 of the Constitution stipulated that "freedom of religion and belief and freedom of religious observance are guaranteed, provided that they do not conflict with the provisions of the Constitution and legislation and are not incompatible with public order and morals." Articles 47 through 56 of the Constitution provided for an elected National Assembly, but its powers were to be defined by the Revolutionary Command Council. Elections for the Assembly took place for the first time in June 1980. Subsequent National Assembly elections were held every four years, and 15 percent of the elected members were women.

This constitution, with its many positive articles on citizenship, did not stop Saddam's regime from violating human rights. The same situation is being created now. Under the new constitution, the militias of the parties heading the government are involved in massive daily violations of Iraqis' human rights, carried out with the blessing of the US-led occupation. That is why most Iraqi women feel that the constitution is not their issue. The constitution should be a development of previous constitutions written under various Iraqi states since the writing of the first in 1925. To do that, one must be free of today's fears and able to enjoy basic human rights, such as walking safely in the streets. Iraqis cannot. Furthermore, the schedule needs to be set by the people themselves and not enforced and imposed by occupation forces.

In this light, let us examine the apparent well-meaning concerns and the main campaigning issue of the US- and British-funded women's organizations, such as WAFDI,[54] the Iraqi Women's Network, and Friends of Democracy, in relation to the constitution. These organizations oppose the enshrining of shari'a into family law and call to remove Article 41 from the Iraqi Constitution, an article that stipulates "all Iraqis are free to abide by a personal status system according to their religions, denominations, beliefs or choices, which would be regulated by law."

Most if not all constitutions in Arabic countries, including the most secular, are either explicitly based on shari'a, or state that nothing should be contrary to shari'a. This is a statement about cultural identity, and by itself has few concrete applications. Shari'a laws are applied under widely varying interpretations of Islam, differ drastically from Saudi Arabia to Tunisia, and offer no single source of interpretation because Islam has multiple schools of *ijtihad* (interpretations). The interpretations range from Salafism to the moderate Muslim Brotherhood. The first calls for the return to an Islam of the venerable forebears, dictating that woman's place is at home to produce and look after child and husband. The second encourages women to take part in public life, including political participation.

Most Iraqi women try to cope sensitively with the predicament of occupation and the rise of reactionary practices affecting their rights and way of life. The problem in Iraq today is not Islam. What we have on the ground, rather, are political parties veiling their collaboration with the occupation; they are subservient to the policy of empire and to religious loyalty, not so much to Islam as to its sectarian subdivisions. Ironically, even the Communist Party is wearing this veil.

Let us dispel a few myths about secularism and symbols such as the dress code. Iraq is often described as a secular country. This was widely accepted at face value following the 1958 Revolution, which popularized the Communist Party. The truth is, beyond the immediate political tides and flows, Iraqis were and remain the proud carriers of Islam, but with their own interpretation that can best be described as the culture of Islam.[55] This applies across the political and class spectrums, to the secular Left as much as to moderate Islamists and nationalists. For the majority of Iraqis, Islam has never been a slogan or a banner. They needed neither the *i'mama* (turban) or *hijab* (a scarf to cover the hair) to prove their identity, religion, or sect. Islam has been the foundation of their cultural identity. Like history, Iraqis carry it within themselves as part of their lives, often without advertising it in the shape of a beard or head cover.

The Qur'an, on which Islam is based, is more than just a holy book. It is also a powerful cultural link unifying over a billion Muslims, about one fifth of the population of the earth. Through its language, 300 million Arabic-speaking people network and communicate, increasingly through access to satellite stations and the Internet.

The Qur'an has saved and preserved the beauty of the language, and Islam has produced a civilization of stunning beauty and advanced human achievement at all levels and aspects of life. Contrary to misconceptions in the West, the Qur'an establishes universal values of respect for elderly men and women, and care and respect for mothers; it encourages wisdom, generosity, tolerance, and knowledge. It celebrates innate moral values of *al rahma* (kindness) and forgiveness. It expressly prohibits the killing of noncombatants: women, children, the aged, even trees. It is these values, rather than punishments and dress codes, that Islam represents for so many Iraqis.

Certainly, the Qur'an requires Muslim women to behave and dress modestly, but these strictures apply equally to men. Only one verse refers to the veiling of women (*Ayat al hijab*),[56] stating that the Prophet's wives should be behind a hijab[57] when his male guests converse with them. Some modernists claim that this does not apply to women in general and was particular to the situation at a time when unruly early followers needed to be taught respect for privacy. Reason (*aql*) is mentioned in the Qur'an 49 times, learning (*'lm*) 108 times, and kindness (*rahma*) over 300 times. So why have all these contributions been ignored, and debate centered on only one image and one issue, the hijab?

Polygamy, already only acceptable in the Qur'an under conditions of equity, was made extremely difficult under the Iraqi 1958 Code. That code also granted child custody to the mother in case of divorce, and prohibited repudiation and marriage under the age of sixteen. Inheritance laws are similar in all Muslim and Arabic countries, guaranteeing that all offspring and dependents have their share. The inheritance shares are governed by strict laws that stipulate that daughters inherit half the male share, even after marriage, and that the wife inherits a fixed share of a deceased husband's estate. This was a revolutionary advancement for women at the time of Muhammad, when women were denied inheritance altogether. It also means, for example, that at any given time, at least a third of all wealth in any Muslim country is owned by women. Moreover it has been the case under Islamic laws for over fifteen centuries to insure that any money or property owned by women is theirs to keep, and that they are not obliged to share it with their menfolk. Similarly, in marriage, a woman's salary is hers and cannot be appropriated by her husband unless she consents.

This is by no mean a justification of ill practices against women in countries claiming Islam as the source of law. In fact, there is a lively debate among Muslim women, feminists and others, about regaining the true stand of Islam toward women through genuine dialogue. I agree with Iraqi sociologist Sana al-Khayyat that "Islam, in theory at least, is not a religion which can be considered to be anti-women, or which goes contrary to women's best interests in a whole variety of ways. It is the adulteration or corruption of Islam which so often militates against women's interests, so much so that religion has been a tool in the hands of those who have wished to control women."[58]

It's true that certain juristic interpretations have contributed to the already existing traditions discriminating between the sexes, in order to preserve a patriarchal order for the family and society. However, in order to understand women's struggle within Iraqi society, it is important to remember that Islam is an essential part of our cultural identity and should continue to be an integral part of the organic development of society as a whole.

The occupation's brutality, its dependence on client parties using Salafite sectarian Islam as a veil (I use the term "Salafite" to describe both the Sunni and Shi'a fundamentalists, though it is usually associated with Sunni), the collapse of the state, the bloodshed and atmosphere of terror—all these have contributed to the fast decline in citizenship rights. Therefore it is impossible to deal with shari'a in relation to women's rights alone, no matter how important women's rights are. It has to be dealt with within the harsh reality of occupied Iraq and the Islam-based sectarian divide which has been used politically to paralyze and render impotent all proper functioning of society, especially so far as it relates to women.

Iraqi women know that the enemy is not Islam. There is a strong antipathy toward anyone trying to conscript women's issues to the racist "War on Terror" targeted against the Muslim world. Most Iraqi women do not regard traditional society, exemplified by the neighborhood and extended family, however restrictive at times, as the enemy. In fact, it has in practice been the protector of women and children, of their physical safety and welfare, and this despite lowest-common-denominator demands on dress and personal conduct. The enemy is the collapse of the state and civil society. And the culprit is the foreign military invasion and occupation.

‖ Life Under Occupation

Life under occupation is bleak. A dismantled state, a powerless government confined to the fortified Green Zone, corruption, the absence of law and order—the resulting chaos makes the notion of citizenship here impossible.

Independent Iraqi women activists, like many women's rights campaigners in other Arabic countries, have always used the framework of citizenship as an effective tool for addressing their unequal access to public spaces. Four years of occupation have proven that Iraqi women's rights are increasingly and dramatically deteriorating. Women who struggled for many decades against the dictatorship report that today is worse than yesterday, which was worse than the day before. For the most part, they're neither Ba'athists, nor radicals or fundamentalists. They are outraged to see their country's resources robbed while they live in slums, and they lack the slightest say in the political process. They despair at the uncertainty in their lives.

The looting of the country by Halliburton, Bechtel, and other contractors, and by local subcontractors and mercenaries, is taking place on a massive scale, and involves many politicians, some of them women. Transparency International, a Berlin-based organization that monitors official graft, patronage, and bribery, lists Iraq as the world's third most corrupt nation behind Haiti and Myanmar. Iraq's top anticorruption watchdog, a high-profile judge whose efforts have been hailed by Americans as one of the few bright spots in the country, is himself the target of a corruption probe. He has pushed for the prosecution of several former ministers, including female cabinet ministers and officials. Corruption is costing the country billions of dollars. The Kurdish Regional Government (KRG), riddled with corruption and nepotism, is a clear example of the widening gap between political parties claiming to represent the people and the people themselves. The KRG was allocated 17 percent of the estimated $41 billion of Iraqi revenue for 2007. Since 2003, it has received billions from Iraqi national revenues and international donors, yet the KRG has failed to provide the people with their basic needs. Most live with only two hours of electricity per day.[1]

In the fourth year of occupation, the "security operation" means military operations by US-led troops, air strikes, indiscriminate random shooting, armed robberies and kidnappings by criminal gangs (at times in police or army uniforms), and raids on homes by masked men arriving in official cars to collect members of a family or to kill them on the spot. It means the eviction of families from neighborhoods as part of ethnic, sectarian, or political cleansing, turning hundreds of thousands into refugees. It means that Iraqis are living with no protection or legal redress, in a general climate of hostility between political parties within and outside the occupation-linked government.

Shaista Aziz is an aid worker, married to Dr. Salam Ismael, the former chief of junior doctors in Baghdad. She witnessed firsthand the brutal US-led attack on the city of Fallujah where her husband was working as a doctor. She went to Baghdad with her husband in January 2007 to help her mother-in-law, whose only brother was killed by militia, and whose cousin had gone missing. She gives this vivid picture of how it feels in occupied Baghdad, providing the kind of information you don't read in the newspapers in New York or London:

> Baghdad is like a ghost city, most of its desperate 6.5 million inhabitants are imprisoned in their homes, it's simply too dangerous to venture out. After sunset hardly anyone leaves the house. Some people have between 15 minutes to 1 hour electricity per day supplied by the national grid; we were lucky enough to be able to afford a generator, but many people have to get through their days on this limited supply of electricity and at this time of year it's freezing cold in Baghdad and people have no way of heating their homes.

At night you hear the continual crackle of gunfire and rockets being launched. U.S. helicopters fly above the skies day and night, in some areas they fly very low, a few inches off the roofs of the houses so the house is constantly vibrating. As they fly above, U.S. soldiers drop heat-detecting objects to try and divert the missiles that are being fired in their direction by insurgents, fighters, militia, and whoever.

There wasn't a minute in the day when I felt safe or secure; bullets are fired at houses by militia, and the U.S./Iraqi military or militia can enter your house at anytime and arrest your son brother father and you have very little idea if and when you might see them again.

One night a group of U.S. soldiers arrived at our house without any warning. They were trying to establish if we were militia and if we had guns. My elderly father-in-law pointed to the windows of the house where a few weeks ago armed militia had fired live rounds from a machine gun into the house; one of the bullets missed my sleeping sister-in-law's head by a few inches. The soldiers then asked my father-in-law if he wanted a gun and insisted that they would give him a weapon if he wanted one. He told them that all he wanted was for them to leave him and the family alone.[2]

In order to understand Iraqi women's priorities under occupation, it is important to identify the complexity of their situation, and to appreciate it beyond a Western feminist point of view.

It is rare for an Iraqi woman to live on her own as a matter of choice. The adult female is almost always a part, and often the center, of a household of five to ten people of all ages. The basic unit of the traditional Iraqi family is the extended family, to which the nuclear family is attached. The gains in women's education and opportunities for work outside the home during most of the twentieth century were leading toward a Western model of nuclear and smaller families. But strong, countervailing cultural currents emerged, and the 1990s sanctions completely reversed this trend. The extended family allows women to have more children, even if they continue to work outside the home, as child care is shared by aunts and grandmothers. The family, though its members may have different sectarian, ethnic, and political backgrounds, remains the primary unit of loyalty.

Today, more than ninety women become widows each day due to continuing violence countrywide.[3] The Ministry of Women's Affairs says that there are at least three hundred thousand widows in Baghdad alone, and a further one million throughout the country, and that the numbers are rising daily as men continue to disappear. Families are left without support. Widows have few resources at their disposal.

Since the announcement by President Bush of "mission accomplished" in 2003, 650,000 Iraqi civilians have been killed. The physical survival of families in scores of areas has been threatened by a series of massacres, in military operations by the US-led forces and in attacks by armed groups.[4]

Palestinian refugees have not been spared. Some of them have been made refugees for the second time. Palestinians arrived in Iraq in three waves—in 1948, 1967, and the 1990s—and were given subsidized housing, the right to work, and, like all Iraqis, free education and health care. Under the occupation, they have been targeted by militias, their houses have been raided, and men and women have been arrested, tortured, and killed. The UN Commission on Human Rights (UNCHR) reports that Palestinians have been forced to pay thousands of dollars to Iraqi security forces for protection. Most of their identity papers have expired, and the Iraqi government refuses to give extensions, since "Palestinians are seen as insurgents or trouble makers."[5]

Massacres, or "mistakes" as they are frequently described by US-UK officials, have been common under occupation, and generally follow the same pattern: kill, try to cover up the crime, then issue a statement blaming it on "insurgents." Here are some examples of underreported crimes:

THE QA'IM WEDDING MASSACRE: In May 2004, Americans bombed the village of Mukaradeeb, killing forty-two members of the Rakat and Sabah families.[6] Mrs. Shihab, thirty, was one of the few in the Rakats' house who survived the night. She spoke from her bed in the emergency ward at Ramadi General Hospital, sixty miles west of Baghdad: "The bombing started at 3 a.m. We went out of the house and the American soldiers started to shoot at us. They were shooting low on the ground and targeting us one by one," she said. She ran with her youngest child in her arms and her two young boys, Ali and Hamza, close behind. As she crossed the fields, a shell exploded close to her, fracturing her legs and knocking her to the ground. She lay there and a second round hit her on the right arm. By then her two boys were on the ground. "I left them because they were dead," she said. One, she saw, had been decapitated by a shell. "I fell into the mud and an American soldier came and kicked me. I pretended to be dead so he wouldn't kill me. My youngest child was alive next to me."[7]

When reporters asked Brigadier General Mark Kimmitt, deputy director of operations for the US military in Iraq, about the killing, he said "We estimate that around forty were killed. But we operated within our rules of engagement."[8]

HADITHA: A statement issued on November 20, 2005, by a US Marine Corps spokesman from a marine base in Ramadi said, "A U.S. Marine and 15 civilians were killed yesterday from the blast of a roadside bomb in Haditha. Immediately following the bombing, gunmen attacked the convoy with small arms fire. Iraqi army soldiers and Marines returned fire, killing eight insurgents and wounding another."

The truth, however, was revealed two months later. What happened in Haditha has been described as the Iraqi My Lai, and the details of the slaying of the civilians contradicted those from the US military statement. Victims "included children and the women who were trying to shield them, the girls killed inside Khafif's house were ages 14, 10, 5, 3 and 1, according to death certificates."[9]

According to eyewitnesses, the marines went on a rampage in Haditha, an agricultural town of about ninety thousand inhabitants on the banks of the Euphrates northwest of Baghdad, after one of their comrades was killed. An Iraqi journalist, who filmed the aftermath of the massacre with the Hammurabi human rights organization, also recorded eyewitness accounts. Twelve-year-old Safa Younis, who lived in one of three houses where troops came in and indiscriminately killed eight people, including Safa's five siblings, aged two to fourteen, said:

> "They knocked at our front door and my father went to open it. They shot him dead from behind the door and then they shot him again. Then one American soldier came in and shot at us all. I pretended to be dead and he didn't notice me."

In another house, seven people, including a child and his seventy-year-old grandfather were killed. Four brothers, aged twenty-four to forty-one, died in a third house. Eyewitnesses said they were forced into a wardrobe and shot. Outside on the street, US troops are said to have gunned down four students and a taxi driver they had stopped at a roadblock set up after the bombing.[10]

ISHAQI: About sixty miles north of Baghdad, on March 15, 2006, US troops rounded up and deliberately shot eleven people in a house, including five children and four women, before blowing up the building, according to Iraqi police and eyewitnesses.[11] In their initial statement, the US military claimed that while they were targeting an al-Qaeda supporter, the building collapsed under heavy fire, killing four people. A video obtained by the BBC contradicted this account. Under public pressure, especially after the Haditha massacre, a US investigation was carried out, concluding that "the ground force commander, while capturing and killing terrorists, operated in accordance with the rules of engagement governing our combat forces in Iraq."[12]

There are more underreported mass deaths which are a result of indiscriminate US shelling, often due to long-range action. In November 2006, medical officials in Ramadi reported that shelling had killed thirty-one civilians, mostly women and children.[13] Mercenaries, death squads, and militias, acting on behalf of sectarian and ethnic political parties involved in the "democratic" political process, are also clearly responsible for the wide-scale killing of civilians.[14] Bodies are found across the country, often handcuffed, blindfolded, bullet-ridden. Often unrecognizable, they are sometimes found dumped at roadsides. The morgue in Baghdad cannot cope with the increasing number of bodies, so it is burying them immediately once photographs have been taken to show bereaved women looking for their missing husbands, fathers, and brothers. In October 2006, a particularly bloody month for Iraqi civilians, about 1,600 bodies were turned in at the Baghdad central morgue, according to its director, Dr. Abdul-Razaq al-Obaidi. The city's network of morgues, built to hold 130 bodies at most, now holds more than 500 at any given time. In other cities, morgues refuse to accept more bodies. Men are tattooing their thighs with names and phone numbers, fearful that if they are killed, they will be buried before their bodies are identified.[15]

■ ■ ■

A total of 254 journalists and media assistants have been killed since the start of the war, and 51 have been kidnapped.[16] By June 2007, 220 doctors had been killed and more than 10,000 had fled Iraq. Thousands of Iraq's best-educated academics, doctors, and other professionals have been forced to flee the country, taking with them the intellectual capital for building a stable, democratic, and free nation. The present government has done little to ensure their safety since it took office.[17] Reporting of crimes against professionals and intellectuals has been scarce, but here are some cases:

- In the northern town of Hawijah, near Kirkuk, on October 27, 2006, gunmen broke into the house of thirty-eight-year-old Halima Ahmed Hussein al-Juburi, the head of the human rights organization Maternity and Childhood, and shot her dead in front of her three children.[18]
- In the al-Doura district of Baghdad, on October 27, 2004, Liqa Abdul Razaq, an anchor on al-Sharqiya TV, was shot with her two-month-old baby.
- The Iraqi journalist Raeda Mohammed Wageh Wazzan, of the regional public television station Iraqiya, was found dead on February 25, 2005, five days after she and her son were kidnapped by masked gunmen in the center of the northern city of Mosul. She was shot in the head.
- Layla al-Saad, Dean of Law at Mosul University, was murdered in her home on June 23, 2004.
- Maha Ibrahim, editor in chief at Baghdad TV, was killed on July 3, 2005. She was shot by US military gunfire.
- On February 22, 2006, gunmen killed Atwar Bahjat, a novelist and correspondent for al-Arabiya TV, as she was reporting from Samarra.

- On September 13, 2006, the body of Safaa Ismail Inad, a journalist at *al-Watan* newspaper, was found near Sadr City in eastern Baghdad.[19]
- Nakshin Hama Rashid, thirty-one, an anchor on the Kurdish-language television station Atiaf, was murdered in her car along with her driver, in the center of Baghdad on October 29, 2006.[20]
- On November 15, 2006, Fadia Mohammed Ali was killed with her driver by gunmen as she was driving to work in Mosul.

None of these crimes has been investigated by occupation forces or the puppet regime. Occupation troops, contractors, diplomats, and those who work for them are immune against prosecutions under new Iraqi law, according to Order 17. Issued by the office of the administrator of the CPA on June 26, 2003, the order states, "In accordance with international law, the CPA, Coalition forces and the military and civilian personnel accompanying them, are not subject to local law or the jurisdiction of local courts. . . . Foreign Liaison Missions and their personnel enjoy immunity from Iraqi legal proceedings."

Long-promised freedom of the press and speech have not materialized since "liberation." In fact, silencing journalists has become the best guarantee to cover up crimes, abuses, and violations of human rights. Journalist Gulshan al-Bayati, *al-Hayat's* correspondent in Tikrit, was arrested on September 11, 2006, for criticizing the US occupation of Iraq in her articles.[21] Newspapers and television stations are closed for "inciting violence." Al-Jazeera, al-Arabiya, and al-Sharqiya, the Iraqi channel, are among them. Clearly, reporting murder is seen as inciting violence.

In fact, reporting corruption in the Kurdish region, which has been spared much of the bloodshed engulfing other parts of Iraq, is considered to be a crime. Freedom of the press under the KRG is nominal, and journalists do not question or criticize the government controlled by the two nationalist parties, for the fear of persecution. The security forces of the

KDP and the PUK are quick to silence voices of dissent. On December 1, 2005, Amnesty International took up the case of the abducted Kurdish writer and human rights advocate Dr. Kamal Sayid Qadir, who was abducted in Arbil by Parastin, KDP's intelligence forces, on November 23, 2005, and has been illegally detained. In December 2005, he was sentenced to thirty years imprisonment for "defamation." He had published articles on the Internet that were critical of the KDP leadership.[22] He was released only after a worldwide campaign led by independent Iraqis (not only Kurds). In Erbil, police arrested journalists Shaho Khalid and Dilaman Salah for reporting a student strike in Setaqan Quarter. After their release, they demanded an apology from the police whom they alleged had assaulted them.[23] The Kurdistan Journalists Syndicate (KJS) proposed a new program to safeguard the dignity of journalists, but many journalists still complain that the KJS has failed to protect their rights in the face of harsh treatment by the government. "I believe if the KJS is there to protect my rights as a journalist and defend me, then they are almost nonexistent, because they mainly represent political parties in the region," Rahman Gharib, correspondent for the prominent *Hawlati Weekly* published in Kurdistan, told IPS.[24] In the course of covering mass demonstrations and strikes that engulfed large parts of Kurdistan in 2006, Gharib was once detained for three hours and beaten on two occasions by local security forces. The demonstrations were held to protest the regional government's failure to provide basic services.

■ ■ ■

Abuses, torture, and the rape of Iraqi women have been reported for four years now by independent Iraqi organizations. Prostitution among Iraqi girls in Syria, some just twelve years old, is becoming more widespread as the economic situation for Iraqi families continues to deteriorate, and more and more of them flee abroad.[25]

The KRG Human Rights Ministry stated that 239 women had burned themselves in the first eight months of 2006. Authorities in Sulaimaniya documented the highest number of monthly traumatic burn cases in November 2006. A Sulaimaniya hospital source suspected that such cases are underreported because of fear of the social stigma, shame, and possible involvement of family members that are associated with honor crimes. Most cases have been investigated as accidents or suicide attempts. It has been acknowledged by government officials that tribal traditions, chauvinistic interpretations of Islam, and unreasonable societal expectations of women are some of the root causes of honor crimes.[26]

Some female officials who have left office have started talking openly about crimes against women. Aida Ussayran, the former deputy human rights minister, admits, "Of course rape is going on. We blame the militias. But when we talk about the militias, many are members of the police. Any family now that has a good-looking young woman in it does not want to send her out to school or university, and does not send her out without a veil. This is the worst time ever in Iraqi women's lives. In the name of religion and sectarian conflict they are being kidnapped and killed and raped. And no one is mentioning it."[27]

What Aida Ussayran chose not to mention is the responsibility of the occupation authority in establishing a corrupt, sectarian government vested with militias. She also chose not to mention the gang rape of A'beer Qassim Hamza al-Janaby by US troops. A'beer Qassim Hamza was a fourteen-year-old girl who lived with her family in a farm house in Mahmudiyah, twenty miles south of Baghdad. She happened to attract the attention of US soldiers at the checkpoint near her house. Describing the young girl, the family's neighbor said, "She had been told by her parents not to go to school any more because of poor security. . . . She spent most of her time at home cleaning, and in the garden so the American forces saw her many times. She was a beautiful girl, and my wife told me that the

Americans kept watching her. When I told her father, though, he said it was no problem and that she was just a small girl."[28] A'beer was terrified and told her mother when US soldiers made advances towards her. The mother thought that the US soldiers might raid their house that night, so she arranged for A'beer to sleep at the neighbor's house. But it was too late. The killings occurred in the middle of that day. On March 12, 2006, at 2 p.m., the bodies of A'beer's mother, Fakhriyah Taha Muhsin, age thirty-four; her father, Qassim Hamza Raheem, age forty-five; and her sister, Hadeel Qassim Hamza, age five, were found burnt to death. A'beer's skull was smashed and her legs and torso set on fire. Her two young brothers were at school at the time. Her uncle said he found A'beer sprawled dead in a corner, her hair and a pillow next to her consumed by fire, and her dress pushed up to her neck.[29]

A US spokesman initially ascribed the killings to "Sunni Arab insurgents active in the area," contrary to eyewitness reports. On July 10, military authorities disclosed that they had filed capital charges of premeditated rape and murder against four of the five active-duty soldiers in the area. The investigation was conducted after a sergeant in the same platoon revealed the crime during a counseling session following the deaths of two other soldiers in the same regiment. Two of the soldiers were sentenced to life imprisonment in February 2007 after admitting taking part in the gang rape of A'beer.

In court it was revealed that the horrendous crime was premeditated by the soldiers while downing whiskey mixed with energy drinks. "The soldiers decided that A'beer would be an easy target for plans to 'have sex with an Iraqi female' because her father was the only man in the house, Cortez told the military court."[30] Further horrifying details emerged during the investigation and in court. A military investigator described the events that took place in Mahmudiya on March 12, based on an interview that he had with one of the accused soldiers.

Special Agent Benjamin Bierce recalled how Specialist James Barker described how the couple and their youngest child were put in another room, while the teenager was kept in the living room. Barker said that he held the girl's hands while Sergeant Paul Cortez raped her or tried to rape her. Barker then switched positions with Cortez and attempted to rape the girl, but said he was not sure if he had done so, Special Agent Bierce told the hearing. Some shots were fired in the other room and Private Steven Green emerged, saying, "They're all dead. I just killed them." Green put down an AK-47 assault rifle and raped the girl while Cortez held her down, the court heard. Bierce said Green then picked up the weapon and shot the girl once, paused, and shot her several more times. Kerosene from a lamp was poured over the girl and someone—it was not clear whom—set her alight.[31]

A'beer's rape and murder is neither incidental nor aberrant. (It was declared a symptom of one US soldier's "personality disorder.") Rather, it is part of a pattern that includes the behavior at Abu Ghraib, as well as the Haditha, Ishaqi, and Qa'im massacres. This pattern serves a strategic function beyond indiscriminate revenge; it fosters the collective humiliation, intimidation, and terrorizing of Iraqi people, a classic colonial maneuver.

On October 19, 2005, Freedom Voice, an Iraqi human rights society, reported the rape of three women from the Saad Bin Abi Waqqas neighborhood in Tal Afar after a US raid. The rape by soldiers took place inside the women's house after the arrest of their male relatives. Medical sources in the town said that one of the women died. A US commander ordered some soldiers detained, and no more was heard of this.

Within days after US troops began Operation Law and Order, the "surge" plan announced by the Bush administration on January 10, two courageous Iraqi women appeared on television to speak about their rapes by Iraqi troops, for the first time in the Arab and Muslim world. The first was twenty-year-old Sabrin al-Janabi (the initial alias for Zainab al-Shummary); the second was Wajda, a mother of eleven from Tal Afar, the northern city. After tearful statements were aired by al-Jazeera, media outlets rushed to describe the rapes to fit with the Anglo-American version of the bloodshed in Iraq—as sectarian. The BBC reported: "The 20-year-old married Sunni woman says she was taken from her home in Baghdad to a police station, where she was accused of helping insurgents—and then raped by three policemen." The report was careful to remind its listeners that the Baghdad police are predominantly Shi'a.[32]

Immediately Prime Minister Nouri al-Maliki, not known for his quick response to the plight of Iraqi women, issued a statement calling the woman a liar and a criminal, and claimed that she was not attacked. He fired an official who had called for an international investigation and who'd described the rape as a "horrific crime," demanding rewards for the officers Zainab accused of raping her. The deputy interior minister, Hussein Ali Kamal, said the allegation by Zainab was unlikely because "something like this could not happen because Iraqi forces are operating with U.S. forces at all times."

Wajda was the second victim raped by Iraqi police when they stormed into her home at the northern city of Tal Afar during Operation Law and Order. In an official statement, Brigade General Nijm Abdullah said that the attack took place during a search for weapons and insurgents. According to Abdullah, a lieutenant and three enlisted men denied the charge but later confessed after they were confronted by the woman, a Turkmen.

In late December 2006, three female students from Mustansiriya University were kidnapped by militias. Despite the payment of ransom, their bodies were found in a morgue on December 22, bearing signs of rape and torture. Official sources denied the incident, but students from the University confirmed it did take place.[33]

The rapes of A'beer, Zainab, and Wajda are just a few of many cases documented by Iraqi human rights organizations and the UN Assistance Mission for Iraq (UNAMI). According to Iraqi MP Muhamad al-Dainey in a recent interview on al-Sharqiya, 1,053 documented cases of rape by the occupation forces, militias, and police have taken place in Iraq since 2003.[34]

■ ■ ■

House raids and random arrests are features of the new Iraq. Women and children, though not always arrested themselves, are victims as well. The raids exhibit a general pattern, which was summarized in a February 2004 report by the International Committee of the Red Cross:

> Arresting authorities entered houses usually after dark, breaking down doors, waking up residents roughly, yelling orders, forcing family members into one room under military guard while searching the rest of the house and further breaking doors, cabinets, and other property. They arrested suspects, tying their hands in the back with flexicuffs, hooding them, and taking them away. Sometimes they arrested all adult males in the house, including elderly, handicapped, or sick people. Treatment often included pushing people around, insulting, taking aim with rifles, punching and kicking, and striking with rifles. Individuals were often led away in whatever they happened to be wearing at the time of arrest—sometimes pyjamas or underwear. . . . In many cases personal belongings were seized during the arrest with no receipt given. . . . In almost all incidents documented by the ICRC, arresting authorities provided no information about who they were, where their base was located, nor did they explain the cause of arrest. Similarly, they rarely informed the arrestee or his family where he was being taken or for how long, resulting in the de facto disappearance of the arrestee for weeks or even months until contact was finally made.[35]

Within months of the occupation of Iraq, complaints surfaced of human rights violations in prisons administered by occupation authorities. It took almost a year—and the publication of photographs of horrific incidents of torture in Abu Ghraib—before the world began to heed the voices of the detainees and those trying to defend them.[36]

Today, tens of thousands of Iraqis are still languishing in prison without being charged with a crime. Both the US-led occupation forces and the Iraqi police "deny detainees their right to challenge the lawfulness of their detention before a court. Some of the detainees have been held for over two years without any effective remedy or recourse; others have been released without explanation or apology or reparation after months in detention, victims of a system that is arbitrary."[37] The North American press started investigating the related legal issues late in 2006, with headlines such as "Iraqi Justice System is in Tatters."[38] The Kurdish area, which has been promoted as a model of democracy for Iraq, is not much better. Human Rights Watch issued a report detailing torture and abuses in security prisons in the Kurdish area. It found a consistent pattern of abuse involving detainees being subjected to beatings and stress positions, and allegations of electric shock torture. The security prisons under investigation are run by security forces known as Asayish, which are attached to the two main Kurdish political parties and are outside the authority of the Kurdistan Regional Government and its interior ministry.[39]

Iraqi women have been caught up in this sweep of detentions, languishing in Abu Ghraib and other prisons. In addition to suffering the same hardships as male inmates, the women endure another plight: silence. First, the denial by occupation authorities that there are female detainees at all; and second, silence from the women's own families because of the stigma surrounding the arrest and detention of a woman. For most Iraqis, the horrifying photos of Abu Ghraib signify not only the abuse and torture of the inmates but also the nightmarish reality of what has not been photographed or published: the torture and rape of their daughters, sisters, and mothers.

Numerous human rights organizations have reported the presence, "for security reasons," of female detainees in many prisons throughout Iraq. [40] There remains considerable uncertainty about the number of female detainees in Iraq, but estimates of the number of Iraqis arrested since the invasion in March 2003 range from thirty thousand to one hundred thousand. Humanitarian organizations, including the International Committee of the Red Cross, Red Crescent, and Amnesty International, say they have documented hundreds of complaints of torture, false imprisonment, and murder by coalition forces. [41]

It was a rare occasion when Anne Clwyd, Tony Blair's personal envoy to Iraq, was moved to speak out about human rights violations under occupation when she learned that a seventy-year-old woman was ridden like a donkey by US troops in one Iraqi prison. [42] Inside Iraq, occupation authorities suppress information about female detainees to avoid Iraqi outrage and to give the Iraqi people the impression that the occupation troops respect local traditions, especially with regard to the sensitive status of women. [43] Apart from cases of well-known detainees like Dr. Huda Saleh Ammash, a member of the Ba'ath regime, and Dr. Rihab Taha, a scientific researcher, Iraqi governments have denied the existence of female detainees, fearing a backlash from the country's traditionally conservative society. [44]

Ali al-Qeisi—the man whose photograph from Abu Ghraib showed him with a black hood over his head, standing on a box, with electric cords on his hands—recalls his anguish at hearing the screams and cries of female detainees. "Their food was brought into their cells by naked men," he relates, adding, "We felt helpless as we listened to their screams, unable to do anything but pray to God Almighty." [45]

Suheib Baz, a cameraman for al-Jazeera TV, told the *Independent* that he had personally seen a twelve-year-old girl being tortured: "She was naked, and crying out to me for help while being beaten." He also relates that prison wardens would photograph these horrors. [46]

The denial of the occupation authorities conflicts with statements made by Muntazar al-Samarrai, the Iraqi general formerly in charge of special forces, who revealed the existence of nine secret detention centers. He also said there are two detention centers for women in Baghdad where "female prisoners are tortured and raped."[47]

According to Seymour Hersh, writing in the New Yorker, General Antonio Taguba said that he saw "a video of a male American soldier in uniform sodomizing a female detainee." The video was not made public in any of the subsequent court proceedings, nor has there been any public government mention of it. Such images would have added an even more inflammatory element to the outcry over Abu Ghraib.[48]

US officials have admitted detaining Iraqi women in order to convince male relatives to provide information. It has been reported that many of the women detained by US forces are the wives or relatives of senior Ba'ath Party officials or suspected militants, and that interrogators have threatened to kill these detainees. Five former detainees told their lawyers they had been beaten while in custody. One said she had been raped and knifed by a US soldier. In May 2004, the US colonel in charge of a prison's detention facilities said that the five women remaining there were kept in solitary confinement for twenty-three hours a day, with only a Qur'an for company. A former Abu Ghraib detainee alleged that a twelve- or thirteen-year-old girl was brought into the prison, stripped naked, and beaten while her brother and other prisoners heard her screams from their cells.[49]

The female minister of state Fatin Mahmoud is one of the few government officials who have admitted the presence of women detainees, and urged the ministries of the interior and defense, and the US occupation troops, to abide by international law when dealing with them. Her call, in fact, was the first official admission that the number of women in various detention centers and prisons has been increasing and that their conditions are worsening. "There are many women in jail," she said, contradicting earlier Iraqi and US reports that there are no women in detention centers under their control. However, within a few hours, she had to withdraw her statement.[50] Such conduct leaves the overwhelming task of uncovering the truth to Iraqi and international human rights organizations, and to the few independent voices still heard in the country.[51]

IV Resistance

On visiting Baghdad with my husband nine months after the occupation began, we found ourselves wondering: Why aren't most people fighting the occupation the way our grandfathers did during the 1920 Revolution? The answer, we came to realize, was "*Nreed njur nifesna awwel*," which literally translates: "We want first to draw breath." Most middle-class Baghdadis whom we met in January 2004 wished for breathing space, to recover some physical strength, and to try to understand the situation with an open mind. They told us that they were against the occupation in principle, but were exhausted and needed a break after a generation of war, sanctions, and death, no matter how short the respite. More than thirteen years of economic sanctions had left the people physically lethargic: one of the reasons for the "swift success" of the invasion. Some had hoped for a measure of truth in the claims made by the United States to justify the invasion, and for a measure of intelligence from the occupiers. Had there been such, the resistance would have followed a different profile and trajectory.

Initially, a wide range of approaches was adopted by Iraqis, apart from the two extremes of directly collaborating with the new status quo and of armed resistance against it. Most people followed the example of the technical staff and civil service personnel who made the pragmatic decision to go on as usual and make do within any official framework given for the country and its services. They wanted badly to ensure that the schools, clinics, courts, and town halls continued to function, even if that meant making concessions. But at times they didn't cooperate absolutely, when changes looked to threaten sovereign or other legal rights. For example, government officers would refuse to verify sales of property, or to issue identity documents or any document with durable effect. Their actions against the state can be seen as analogous to the "go slow" and "work to rule" tactics of trade unions, a level of protest short of striking. Yet other groups, especially outside public service employment, took to peaceful protests and demands through petitions, delegations, demonstrations, or elections in the resurrected professional organizations (however insubstantial these had become under the old regime). Some people protected fugitives and those wanted by the occupiers. Some would support resistance groups with funds or communal protection. The motives for the various forms of direct or indirect acts of resistance were a mixture of patriotism, tribal ties, family obligation, hedging bets on the future, and fear. On the other hand, the occupation and its collaborator regime were offering substantial personal and local gains for services in implementing changes and new laws. The balance between the factors for resistance and collaboration has varied from place to place and over time.

The fourth year has also almost put an end to various aspects of passive and nonviolent resistance, which characterized resistance in the first three years. Occupation has been so brutal, it has left no room for any initiative independent of the political process in the Green Zone or for the development of peaceful opposition.[1]

It is important to remember that armed resistance against occupation is a right under international law.[2] It is also worth emphasizing that, contrary to claims by the occupation and the media that publicize it, the main target of the Iraqi resistance are occupation forces; 75 percent of the recorded attacks have been directed at the occupation, with 17 percent at the Iraqi government forces. (The remaining 8 percent are directed at unspecified civilian targets.) Obviously, the resistance has no press office to provide fact sheets or press releases after every attack on occupation forces. We do know, however, that the average number of attacks has more than doubled in the last year, to about 185 per day; that is, 1,300 per week, and over 5,500 attacks per month.[3]

We know from previous struggles by national liberation fronts, such as those in Vietnam and Algeria, and from our own experience fighting the Ba'ath regime, that Iraqi women are taking part in the fight, although the extent of their role remains undocumented. US military "experts" on counterinsurgency in Iraq may not be a reliable source of the extent of women's involvement in the armed resistance, but they give us an idea of how the occupation perceives women's role within the insurgency. Here is an expert's advice to occupation forces: "Engage the women. Most insurgent fighters are men. But in traditional societies, women are hugely influential in forming the social networks that insurgents use for support. Co-opting neutral or friendly women, through targeted social and economic programs, builds networks of enlightened self-interest that eventually undermine the insurgents. You need your own female counterinsurgents, including inter-agency people, to do this effectively. Win the women, and you own the family unit. Own the family, and you take a big step forward in mobilizing the population."[4]

■ ■ ■

Peaceful political resistance was common in the first two years of the occupation, despite the limited public space. Particularly active were members of the Iraqi National Foundation Congress (INFC), which is similar in its structure and ideas to the African National Congress (ANC) and the Palestine Liberation Organization (PLO). It is an alliance of forces united around one main demand: national liberation. It consists of more than twenty-two political parties and independent organizations, including women's and civil-society groups such as the Society of the Iraqi Jurists and the Association of University Lecturers, which also include female professionals.

The INFC was founded in May 2004, representing people who opposed Saddam's regime and who refused to be part of any process implemented by the occupation to legitimize and prolong its hegemony on Iraqi people and territory. The Congress calls for an immediate withdrawal of occupation troops and for the unity of the Iraqi territory and people against any division based on religious, sectarian, or ethnic divide. It also supports the right to resist the occupation by any means necessary. Thus, the INFC had offered, as early as the first year of the occupation, a genuine Iraqi alternative to the occupation, an alternative which has been increasingly representative of the majority of Iraqi people and their aspirations beyond the "pragmatism" of the sectarian and ethnic political parties of the Green Zone.

The INFC secretary general is Sheikh Jawad al-Khalisi, a prominent Shi'a scholar and the head of the Khalisi School—a university, founded in 1911 by his grandfather, that now combines technology, science, and law studies with theology. Al-Khalisi's grandfather was a distinguished ayatollah who led the Shi'a opposition to the British occupation of the 1920s. Another INFC member is Dr. Muthana al-Dhari, spokesman of the Sunni Association of Muslim Scholars (AMS). The AMS is headed by Hareth al-Dhari, whose great-grandfather Sheikh Dhari assassinated Colonel Gerald Leachman, an arrogant and brutal British officer during the 1920s. The INFC spokesman is Wamidh Nadhmi, a professor of political science at Baghdad University and a veteran secular Arab nationalist.

At its second national conference in May 2005, the Congress emphasized its support for "all possible means to end the occupation," stating that "a declaration of an unconditional schedule of withdrawal of foreign troops from Iraq is the minimal condition for us to participate in the writing of the constitution, in the coming elections, and in any other political process." The INFC members made use of very limited public space to represent the entire political arena and voice their opposition to occupation in a peaceful manner. They also played an active role calling for reconciliation among different political factions, unifying people whenever the occupation and its puppets tried to plant seeds of sectarian and ethnic schism among them. They were the first to condemn terrorist attacks on innocent Iraqis and public property—declaring that it is totally alien to the history and practices of Iraqi people—and the manufactured feuds that sow seeds of strife and ethnic, religious, and sectarian hatreds.

They hold the occupation forces, the interim Governing Council, and the transitional government responsible for following the policy of divide and rule, encouraging sectarian and ethnic divisions, and imposing them on all the institutions they have created.[5] The INFC is calling for the formation of independent local and national committees to monitor sectarian crimes and attacks, to investigate the reasons behind them, and to offer guidance and help. Their minimum demand was ignored by the transitional government.

Faced with the ruthlessness of the occupation, the risks have become high for those involved in resistance and also for those surrounding them, since the occupiers and their government quickly established practices of collective punishment in retaliation for anti-occupation activity. Political work has had little chance to develop, and most members have either had to leave Iraq and continue their work in exile, go underground, or keep a low profile.

In the early days of the occupation, women demonstrated together with men or occasionally on their own, usually to demand the release of male relatives detained in various Anglo-American camps, to protest their dismissal from jobs, or to demand to be allocated widows' pensions. Students and teachers demonstrated peacefully to protest the US troops' raids on some colleges and universities and, in one instance, to seek the release of three women who were detained when the Technology University in Baghdad was raided.[6]

In the early months of 2005, thousands of people demonstrated in Baghdad to demand the release of detainees. In fact, it was a peaceful demonstration that triggered the Fallujah bloodshed and the subsequent destruction of the city by Anglo-American troops. A group of local people gathered near a school to call for the US troops to leave the building, so that lessons could resume there.[7] The US troops opened fire, killing thirteen civilians. Fallujah is the site of an ancient trading post, was once a capital city (eleventh century A.D.), and contains many religious and modern colleges. Fallujans are generally tribal and religiously conservative, with a particularly dominant privacy code. When occupying soldiers were using night binoculars to peer into houses, the public anger that ensued was inevitable. Similar events involving the British occurred soon after, in the southern town of Majar al-Kabir, when dogs, seen as unclean by Muslims, were used to search houses. Hundreds of people, angered by the searches, followed the soldiers to a marketplace. A demonstration began and shooting broke out. The British soldiers shot and killed four of the demonstrators.[8]

Reviving old social networks has been the Iraqis' main strategy to cope with the collapse of the state and the consequent mounting crises. Most Iraqis distinguish between community-based and civil-society structures, and are aware of the necessary overlaps between them. Extended families, neighborhood and community-based groups in urban areas, clans and tribes, and mosques are obvious visible examples of community structures. On the other hand, teacher-parent associations, local chambers of commerce, lawyers' and other professional unions, and women's and human rights organizations are examples of civil-society structures, distinct from organs of the state. In the absence of the state, some of these groups provide basic services, like running clinics for women and children in different areas. All these structures create networks functioning within the community above the politically manufactured divide.

Throughout the first three years of occupation, mosques played a crucial role as community centers and as places of learning, organizing, helping the poor, and providing advice on social issues. Some mosques acted as suppliers of electricity, buying big generators, or ran classes to educate children unable to reach schools. Mosque loudspeakers are not only used to call for prayer but also to warn local people of a militia attack or the approach of US Humvees, or to broadcast appeals by doctors for supplies or blood donors. Wrapped in their abayas, young female students, teachers, and nurses are the main collectors and distributors of supplies and donations. Now many mosques are under siege by the US military and militias.

Within the neighborhood, families continue the tradition of helping and protecting one another, despite all the forces trying to divide them. When a Sunni family is forced by one of the militias to leave its neighborhood, a Shi'ite family may offer to collect the food ration and to deliver it, despite all the risk involved.[9] When churches or mosques have been destroyed, delegates from the INFC rush to where the incident has taken place, offering protection and trying to reconcile people to ease feelings of bitterness, anger, and revenge.

There is a long tradition of intercommunal cooperation and intermarriage between Sunni and Shi'a, Kurds and Arabs, Muslims and Christians. I asked a Kurdish friend who married an Arab about the plan to divide Iraq into three separate states—a plan that has been entertained by the United States, Britain, and Israel: "Well, first of all they have to divide our bed into two. Second, they have to separate us in different states. . . . But above all, what about our Baghdad? How do you divide a city that is home to Sunni and Shi'a Muslim Arabs, Kurds (a third of Baghdad's inhabitants are of mixed Arab-Kurd marriages), Turkmen, Christians and Sabians?"[10]

■ ■ ■

Iraqi women are learning that the occupation forces are in the country to guard their own interests, not those of the Iraqis. In refusing to take part in initiatives by the US-led occupation or its Iraqi allies, which usually offer material and social advantages, women practice passive resistance. They adopted the same technique against Saddam's despised General Federation of Iraqi Women and managed to undermine the legitimacy of one of the richest and most powerful institutions for women in the Middle East. The majority of them have continued the same strategy under occupation.

Some women's organizations have grown organically within new movements, or independently, unlike the colonial feminist NGOs. Initially, Iraqi political parties were desperate to employ women to boost their own credibility. Nevertheless, most Iraqi women refused to take part and did not welcome the chance to be a "model" for others in the Middle East.

Meanwhile, a few independent organizations chose nonviolent active resistance, having identified their own priorities and timing. They have joined protests, appeals, vigils in front of prisons, and initiatives to set up a definite timetable for withdrawal of foreign troops. They have also helped by joining human rights groups, lecturing at universities, and even writing poetry. This torrent of peaceful activism has been practiced by a broad spectrum of political parties, women's groups, and individuals who oppose the occupation. They have been silenced because they refuse to be confined to the illusive "pragmatic" or "depoliticized" criteria which have become the trademark of some Iraqi political parties collaborating with the occupation.

One of the few women's organizations that existed prior to the invasion and does not fit into the "depoliticized" criteria of US-funded NGOs, but has continued its activism under occupation, is the Iraqi Women's Will (IWW). It was established as a cultural club for women in 2002, a year before the occupation, by the writer, journalist, and activist Hana Ibrahim. Hana, an independent left-wing activist from the 1970s, and mother of three grown children, had managed to steer an independent path during the Ba'ath regime, creating a wide network of contacts spanning academics, journalists, and artists. Hana was also the editor of the weekly newsletter *Gender*, a publication that addressed various problems faced by Iraqi women at home and in the workplace. According to Hana, she managed despite all difficulties to persuade UNICEF to provide the club with funding to open a women's cultural center in Baghdad.

The club started by organizing art exhibitions and poetry evenings, and it soon became clear that men also were eager to attend the literary and cultural events.

Under the occupation, Hana had to establish a new organization:

> When the invaders reached Baghdad in 2003, my friends and I were sleeping at the cultural center in order to protect it. We managed to persuade some of the gunmen to leave us alone. We had 39 paintings by Iraqi women artists to protect, books, furniture as well as the place itself. Then a man I would call Mr. S., who was dressed in an official suit, came in one day in May, along with five other men. They were heavily armed and dressed in military fatigues. Mr S. told us that they were feeling merciful that day, therefore they would spare us if we would leave the building quietly. I tried to argue and reason with them for two hours, to no avail. They claimed to be members of [the party] led by Ahmed Chalabi, and [said] that they came to occupy the center. In the end, we had to leave and they used the building as one of their party's branches.
>
> A few months later, Paul Bremer, the "American president of Iraq," re-claimed the building from Chalabi's men, but instead of offering it back to us, it was made available to an organization called "Women for Women International."
>
> The center was immediately fitted with extravagant furniture and modern computers, but it remained open for only two months.[11]

Hana, along with a few other members of the club, did not give up. They founded IWW, which combines anti-occupation activities with demanding full, equal women's rights. The IWW has no illusions regarding the occupation's promises of democracy and human rights. Hana says: "How absurd when the US-led forces invade Iraq, devastate the fragile infra-structure, destroy our cities, loot our public buildings and dismantle all government's institutions in the name of democracy and human rights. Even more absurd when all is done in the name of women's rights!"[12]

IWW joined the Iraqi National Foundation Congress in June 2004 to campaign within the national liberation framework on economic, politi-cal, and social issues affecting the welfare and future of Iraqi women. The organization's monthly journal, O'oqul (Minds), discusses the difficulties facing women under occupation. They lobby on constitutional issues fac-ing women and are concerned with issues around globalization and the environment. Its projects include campaigning to boycott Israeli goods and organizing art exhibitions and poetry readings.

At the most basic level of community life, despite all the risk involved, members of IWW try their best to attend Majlis al-A'aza to share grief and sympathy with families of the dead, especially from different religious backgrounds, in order to ease sectarian tension at highly volatile times.

Clearly IWW does not fit with the idea of a "depoliticized women's organization," which has been pursued extensively in Palestine and Iraq. In fact, IWW became more politicized, contrary to the seemingly depoliticized nature of the NGOs that formed after the invasion. Hana calls the stance of IWW "openly anti-occupation," which greatly con-trasts with WAFDI's position of pledging unconditional support for the occupation and the American reconstruction project.

The IWW has no outside sources of funds but relies on voluntary work, the support of a few friends, and the sale and subscription of its journal, which is published free as a monthly supplement by a daily newspaper. Their "headquarters" is a room in one of the members' houses. Hana explains:

> We have closed our office and try to continue working while on
> the move. It's getting too dangerous to stay at the same place for

more than few days. We woke up yesterday to the sight of four hanged young men opposite the house. This morning I saw a young man running carrying *samoun* [Iraqi bread]. A car had stopped him at the end of the road. Three men got off the car and shot him in the head. We watched with horror. Waiting . . . hoping for the storm to calm down. I'll send you our report on Haditha massacre and juvenile detainees.[13]

Another homegrown NGO that deals with women and family is Knowledge for Women in Iraqi Society, established in June 2003 by Rashad Zaydan, a pharmacist and mother of four. Its mission emphasizes the role of women within family and society, and aims to relieve the suffering of Iraqi women by providing financial, occupational, medical, and educational resources, in addition to campaigning for human rights, women's rights in particular.

Throughout the country, it has seventy staff and more than three hundred volunteers. It is financed by the participation of its members and the modest income from its projects, accepting only unconditional aid and support from charitable and humanitarian entities."[14] The organization was active during the siege of Fallujah in 2004, helping to provide displaced families with basic needs such as tents, clean water, and fans. In response to the community's demand, it opened a branch there to continue its work.

These two independent organizations differ in character and style of work. The IWW is largely an intellectual and cultural group with a clear political and social outlook, concerned with the preservation of Iraqi national unity and identity while highlighting the issue of women's rights as a human right. IWW has been active within the Iraqi Foundation Congress in formulating the agenda for an uncompromising anti-occupation movement and in influencing public opinion at home and abroad. KWIS, on the other hand, is a charity and practical-help group, concerned with gaining material support for suffering families, whether medicines or funds. It also runs courses in literacy and basic information technology for women and orphans. Both organizations have deep-rooted relationships with traditional values and civil-society units, including mosques and tribes. The essential overlap lies in the stand against the occupation. From the start, IWW joined the anti-occupation demonstrations, including with Sadrists (followers of the Islamist leader Muqtada al-Sadr), but had to draw a line when pressured to wear the hijab, which is seen as an issue of choice for members of the IWW. According to the US military's statements, some women are getting arrested for being "terrorists," or for transporting weapons and explosives.[15] Some women are arrested under the novel charge of being "potential suicide bombers." It is a disturbing development that Iraqis, who traditionally hold life so dear that they won't celebrate an historical figure if he or she commits suicide, are now becoming suicide bombers. Only a few of them have been women.

The first time the world heard of female suicide bombers from Iraq was when an attack was carried out in which three occupation soldiers were killed at a checkpoint northwest of Baghdad on April 3, 2003. Al-Jazeera broadcast separate videotapes of the two women, one saying she was seeking martyrdom and the other threatening a jihad or holy war against American, British, and Israeli infidels.[16]

Some Iraqi women have become radicalized, often due to the loss of a relative or loved one.[17] They refuse to resign themselves to the "inevitable," making the transition from passive to active protest, which has required them to risk their lives. One example is Um Abdallah, aged forty-one, who said, "My husband was killed four months ago by Iraqi forces. Killed alongside him were my son-in-law and his two children. I cannot even remember how many bullets the children had in their bodies. I'm going to be a suicide bomber in the name of God. . . . I will be one of the Iraqis who will take revenge for all suffering that US and Iraqi militaries have caused in the past years, and force them to leave the blessed land of Iraq. I know I will die but for a good reason.[18]

■ ■ ■

Nearly every aspect of Iraqi life has been affected by the occupation, and Iraqis have realized that, at heart, it is their culture that is being targeted: their history, collective memory, values, modes of expression, and ways of life. So cultural resistance has become an essential element in the people's overall resistance to occupation. It implies a striving to continue their own strands of creativity and imagination, despite difficulties and restrictions. It also implies resisting the political edicts and funding structures that enforce the dominance of the occupation's policies and cultural preferences. In other words, cultural resistance is one of the acts of countering or confronting the hegemony of the occupation at its deepest level: the ways in which the occupied Iraqis continue to assert their own identity in terms of history and culture, language and religion.

Through the stages of occupation and its successive puppet governments, cultural resistance has taken various forms. These range from mere survival and continuity of preoccupation practices—for example in handicrafts, music, and paintings—to the production of documentary films with newer and simpler technologies, and from Friday sermons in a mosque pulpit to the use of the electronic media to bypass the occupation force's control of information.

In the aftermath of the Abu Ghraib prison scandal, twenty-five Iraqi artists organized an exhibition to convey their rage, producing a series of sculptures, paintings, and installations. These depicted the horrors of Abu Ghraib and other detention centers under US and British supervision, which have come to symbolize for many Iraqis how the dream of liberation and democracy has turned into the nightmare of occupation and violence. Qassim al-Sabti created a life-size figure of a woman wrapped in a bloodstained white shroud, to symbolize the rape of women detainees in Abu Ghraib. Abdel-Karim Khalil made three sculptures; one of them is a foot-high rendition of the classic hooded figure, the symbol of Abu Ghraib, with his arms outstretched.

In his comments on the exhibition, Khalil touched on the change of the Iraqi artist's role under occupation: "Some artists used to be neutral, but now there are artists, poets, and writers who have all reached the decision that the Americans are destroyers. It has given them a new sense of purpose in art."[19]

Most of Baghdad's galleries are closed, and many artists have fled Iraq during the first three years of occupation. I asked Zeina (not her real name), a journalist who lived in Baghdad and filmed *Iraq: The Women's Story* for the British Channel 4, how Iraqi women were resisting the occupation. Her answer was very short: "Just to survive in Iraq now is resistance."[20] Zeina and a friend, Intisar al-Araiby, a pharmacist at the Yarmouk Teaching Hospital in West Baghdad, worked together on a documentary film in Qa'im,[21] a remote town west of Baghdad on the Euphrates. They both risked their lives during their journey to reach towns that no other journalist could get to unless embedded with US troops. Both have paid a high price for their courage. Both had to leave Iraq with their children, fearing for their lives. Intisar also suffered the loss of her brother, whose body she found in a refrigerator in her own hospital.[22]

Zeina wanted to make the film because the things she saw every day were not seen by the outside world. She longed especially to document the situation of women, however narrow the limits within which she had to work. "I really want to report on the families who are being arrested, on the bodies that are being found, on torture. But either you are a journalist who is working with the Americans—embedded with them—or you jeopardize your life to cover these stories."[23]

Documentary filmmakers like Zeina and Intisar are targeted, as are actors who take part in plays, films, or television series. Muttashar al-

Soudani, a veteran actor who starred in several Iraqi soap operas and plays over three decades, was killed on December 20, 2006. Walid Hassan, a star of a satirical television series that became hugely popular for its dark humor about the country's predicaments under occupation, was killed in Baghdad, in November 2006.[24] Apparently, in the "New Iraq," a sense of humor is considered another terrorist's tool.

In 2003, Maysoon Pachachi, a London-based documentary filmmaker of Iraqi origin, and Kasim Abid, in cooperation with Abid's Iraqi colleagues, founded an independent film and television college in Baghdad.[25] This provided media courses for one to two months, free of charge, for young Iraqi filmmakers, but it had to move to Amman due to the deteriorating security. The school encouraged graduates to produce their own films. Hiba Bassem, a young woman from the northern city Kirkuk, who returned to Baghdad after the invasion to finish her studies at the Academy of Fine Arts, was one of them. Her short film *Baghdad Days* (2005) is a diary of her year in Baghdad, as she tries to find a place to live, looks for work, graduates from college, deals with family problems, and struggles to come to terms with her position as a woman on her own.

While well-known media personalities, singers, and poets are intimidated and silenced, anonymous literary resistance work flourishes. Young people have been inventive in making up new ways to challenge the occupation, and recordings on CDs are replacing some of the missing voices. The Iraqi Artist's Association (IAA) said that nearly 80 percent of the singers during Saddam's era have fled the country and that at least seventy-five singers had been killed since the US-led invasion of Iraq in 2003.[26] On this issue, crisis group Middle East Report noticed that "for increasing numbers of Iraqis, disenchanted with both the U.S. and their own leaders and despairing of their poor living conditions, solace is found in the perceived world of a pious and heroic resistance. CDs that picture the insurrection's exploits can readily be found across the country, new songs glorify combatants, and poems written decades ago during the post–World

War I British occupation are getting a new lease on life. A 1941 poem on Falluja written by Ma'ruf al-Rusafi has been rediscovered. . . . More generally, insurgent videos are widely distributed in mosques and readily available in most Baghdad movie-stores."[27]

Lack of cultural, or indeed any, ordinary contact between the occupiers and Iraqi society was an early measure of the occupation's failure. The extent of this failure is shown by the fact that the US military has managed to recruit only a few Iraqi translators and interpreters, and that some of these have been killed or chased away, are in need of costly protection, or are themselves considered a security risk. The US military finds it increasingly difficult to employ Iraqis whom they can trust and who know the local culture and people.

To invade any country is in itself a hugely complex undertaking by any power. But the total lack of basic knowledge and understanding of Iraqi society or Arab-Muslim culture shown by the United States is extraordinary. For the United States to claim that they can win hearts and minds, and build a democracy that makes Iraq a model for the rest of the Arab world, without knowing the language and culture of the country, seems a bizarre notion by any standard.

Also bizarre is the type of solution being sought for what is now called the "communication problem" in Iraq. The military is resorting to new technologies. They are using handheld voice-translating devices to replace human interpreters in the field and to convert simple English commands into Iraqi Arabic.[28] One member of the US military shares his view on the dilemma. "In years past, there wasn't a great need for the individual soldier to speak a foreign language to do his mission," said Wayne Richards, branch chief for technology implementation at US Joint Forces Command. But in Iraq and Afghanistan, soldiers are increasingly interacting with Iraqi civilians, giving advice at checkpoints or guidance during home searches. "During those door-to-door searches, the soldiers need to be able to calm them down and reassure them," Richards said. "We're fighting for hearts and minds. But if I can't tell her, 'Ma'am, please calm down,' . . . that wouldn't be assuring."[29]

Poetry, whether in classical Arabic or Iraqi dialect, is a powerful tool of cultural resistance which is almost impossible to counter by the occupation. One of our highly respected poets is May Muzaffar, who tries to capture the moments of destruction of her city and the killing of her people, in her series of "Snapshots":[30]

I
Under the ruins which was a city
and the stones which were a home
with the burnt trunks which were trees
and the dried blood which was a person
look there
for under the ruins and the stones and the dust
lie golden ingots uncollected by the invaders.

2
It is not enough to open your eyes
to look about you
to step with care
remember
that within you is a heart liable to explode.

Online resistance is proving increasingly influential at a time when the occupation and its puppets continue to silence independent Iraqi writers, and to make it impossible for foreign journalists to function unless embedded.

Some bloggers have shown themselves as valuable and verifiable sources of reporting from inside Iraq, especially at a time when the much-trumpeted freedom of speech in print and other media has been curbed by bullet or decree. They provide opinions and analysis while documenting the time, place, and details of their harsh reality. At times they have a literary value, expressing deeply felt emotions and articulating fresh and provocative ideas, which are then available to people who would not otherwise have access to such information.

Indeed, through their online diaries or journals of their day-to-day existence, survival, and struggle on various levels, and by virtue of their amateur nature, bloggers are providing the outside world with a candid lens to see beyond conventional reporting, to put faces and names to the often obliterated people of Iraq, and to see the impact of war and occupation on their lives and the people around them.

Riverbend, a young Baghdadi blogger, uses the old Arabic tradition of storytelling to relate how we have been stripped of our right to build our own country:

Yesterday, I read how it was going to take up to $90 billion to rebuild Iraq. Bremer was shooting out numbers about how much it was going to cost to replace buildings and bridges and electricity, etc. Listen to this little anecdote. One of my cousins works in a prominent engineering company in Baghdad—we'll call the company H. This company is well known for designing and building bridges all over Iraq. My cousin, a structural engineer, is a bridge freak. . . . As May was drawing to a close, his manager told him that someone from the CPA (Coalition Provisional Authority) wanted the company to estimate the building costs of replacing the New Diyala Bridge on the South East End of Baghdad. He got his team together, they went out and assessed the damage, decided it wasn't too extensive, but it would be costly. They did the necessary tests and analyses . . . and came up with a number they tentatively put forward: $300,000. This included new plans and designs, raw materials (quite cheap in Iraq), labour, contractors, travel expenses, etc. Let's pretend my cousin is a dolt. Let's pretend he hasn't been working with bridges for over 17 years. Let's pretend he didn't work on replacing at least 20 of the 133 bridges damaged during the first Gulf War. Let's pretend he's wrong and the cost of rebuilding this bridge is four times the number they estimated—let's pretend it will actually cost $1,200,000. Let's just use our imagination.

A week later, the New Diyala Bridge contract was given to an American company. This particular company estimated the cost of rebuilding the bridge would be around—brace yourselves— $50,000,000! Something you should know about Iraq: we have over 130,000 engineers. More than half of these engineers are structural engineers and architects. Thousands of them were trained outside of Iraq in Germany, Japan, America, Britain, and other countries. Thousands of others worked with some of the foreign companies that built various bridges, buildings, and high-ways in Iraq. The majority of them are more than proficient—some of them are brilliant.

Iraqi engineers had to rebuild Iraq after the first Gulf War in 1991, when the "Coalition of the Willing" was composed of over thirty countries actively participating in bombing Baghdad beyond recognition. They had to cope with rebuilding bridges and buildings that were originally built by foreign companies, they had to get around a lack of raw materials that we used to import from abroad, they had to work around a vicious blockade designed to damage whatever infrastructure was left after the war. . . . They truly had to rebuild Iraq. And everything had to be made sturdy, because, well, we were always under the threat of war.

Over a hundred of the 133 bridges were rebuilt, hundreds of buildings and factories were replaced, communications towers were rebuilt, new bridges were added, electrical power grids were replaced . . . things were functioning. Everything wasn't perfect—but we were working on it. So instead of bringing in thousands of foreign companies that are going to want billions of dollars, why aren't the Iraqi engineers, electricians, and labourers being taken advantage of? Thousands of people who have no work would love to be able to rebuild Iraq. . . . No one is being given a chance.[31]

■ ■ ■

International networking has become increasingly important in the Iraqi struggle for liberation and social justice. It is also an important part of the nonviolent resistance. This includes links with the international movements which, in the case of Britain, are represented by the Stop the War Coalition,[32] Voices in the Wilderness (VITW),[33] and Iraq Occupation Focus,[34] and in the case of other countries, by various related or unrelated antiglobalization movements. These links are often based on personal contacts by Iraqis, which have developed during the thirteen years of sanctions and close links with Iraqi exiles. The role of the peace movement in countries that already have troops in Iraq is vital in order to put pressure on their governments to call for the withdrawal of the troops from occupied Iraq. There is also historical continuity with initiatives that started during the US war on Vietnam. One of these is the World Tribunal on Iraq (WTI), which is "a worldwide undertaking to reclaim justice. It aims to record the severe wrongs, crimes and violations that were committed in the process leading up to the aggression against Iraq, during the war and throughout the ensuing occupation, that continue to be widespread to this day."[35] Another is the BRussells Tribunal (BT), a network of individuals who object to the US-led occupation of Iraq and the logic of permanent war imposed by the United States under Bush. The Tribunal works to expose the war crimes, crimes against humanity, and systematic illegality of US wars in and on the Arab world and elsewhere, and to uphold the legitimacy of resistance to imperialism, colonialism, and brutality by all means.[36] The BT has launched an international campaign to create awareness about the systematic killings of Iraqi academics; it is the only worldwide peace network that has Iraqis on both its executive and advisory committees.

Iraqi women led a group of witnesses who travelled to Istanbul June 23–27, 2005, to attend the final session of the World Tribunal on Iraq. They joined international human rights lawyers, professors, writers, reporters, and experts, who came together from all over the world to document the injustices occurring in occupied Iraq. The international jury of conscience at the tribunal listened to testimonies from these women, such as the journalist Hana Ibrahim, chair of Iraqi Women's Will.

In the diaspora, there are a few Iraqi organizations—such as Iraqi Democrats Against Occupation[37] (IDAO), the Iraqi Committee for National Media and Culture (ICNMC), and Solidarity for an Independent and Unified Iraq[38]—active within the international antiwar and peace movements, providing the independent Iraqi voices needed to formulate the strategy to work together based on understanding, equality, and respect. The other aspect of their work is to expose the US-UK media cover-up surrounding the atrocities and massacres committed by the occupation, misleading the public regarding the sectarian divide.

Sectarian strife has been created by the occupation; it is not due to its failure. In fact, the "dormant" sectarian tensions have been nurtured to explode at any moment. And certainly the imposition of sectarian quotas on a secular country has revived moribund sectarian groups.

We are being told repeatedly that the main story in Iraq is that Iraqis are killing Iraqis by the hundreds each day, and that the main question is whether it has yet become a sectarian civil war. But for Iraqis, the presence of occupation troops and the crimes they are committing is the main story, and the question is how to stop them.

Afterword

The exit of occupation troops from Iraq is imminent. For us, the question is no longer when are the troops leaving, but rather how will they deal with the chaos and destruction they created, how will they attempt to compensate the people for their massive losses, and how will they try to build bridges with Iraqi, Arab, and Muslim populations to regain faith in democracy.

There has been a history of opposition to brutality in Iraq, a long line of resistance movements that fought to put an end to all abuses of human rights, torture, violence against women, the death penalty, and public executions. The occupation has crushed that spirit. We, who had dreams of going back home to help rebuild our country, have been joined now in exile by another 2.5 million Iraqis. Hopes to see the "new Iraq" are diminishing with every house demolished, with every school and hospital bombarded, with every family forced to leave home, with every woman widowed. Despair is overtaking us, and we know very well, from the Palestinian tragedy, how volatile despair is when mixed with injustice, and how indiscriminate violence can be in response.

What does the future hold for us? A group of over one hundred Iraqi writers, artists, and academics in exile convened to discuss the future of Iraq and the Middle East. In a letter we delivered to the British government a few months before the invasion, we wrote: "A real change can only be brought about by the Iraqi people themselves within an environment of peace and justice for all the peoples of the Middle East." This continues to be the case, though the circumstances have eroded beyond imagination. What the occupiers have failed to see is that Iraqis who have committed acts of resistance are not terrorists. We are a people willing to risk our lives defending our homes, families, ways of life, history, culture, identity, and resources. We do not hate Americans, though we do loathe their government's greed and brutality, and are willing to defend ourselves against it. We simply believe that Iraq belongs to Iraqis.

I'm often asked the question, "Will you ever go back to Iraq?" It always shocks me because, deep down, I feel like I never left.

—July 2007

Notes

1. "Baghdad not as 'secure' as government claims, residents say." *Azzaman* (October 13, 2008) (in Arabic).

2. Aidan Jones, "Killings force 13,000 Christians to flee Mosul," *Guardian* (October 25, 2008).

3. Maggie Fox, "Satellite images show ethnic cleanout in Iraq," Reuters (September 19, 2008), http://www.reuters.com/article/newsOne/idUSN1953066020080919.

4. Joseph Giordono and Monte Morin, "Soldiers building wall separating Sunnis, Shiites," *Stars and Stripes*, Mideast edition (April 19, 2007).

5. In 2007, UNESCO named Samarra—home to a ninth-century mosque and majestic ruins along the Tigris River—one of its World Heritage Sites.

6. A Pentagon working group issued a 244-page report in September 2007 that proposed a $195 million program to expand the use of iris scans, fingerprints, DNA, and other traditional as well as novel crime lab tools in the wars in Iraq and Afghanistan. See "Fingerprints, eye scans stop suspects in tracks," *USA Today* (November 12, 2007).

7. The Biometric screening process includes an iris scan, fingerprinting, photographing of the face from different angles, and a background check. The iris scan, fingerprinting, and photo portion of the Biometric screening takes about twenty minutes, but it takes up to three days to process the background check. These regulations apply to the media as well. See "Media Credentialing Process," Multi-National Force–Iraq (July 15, 2008), http://www.mnf-iraq.com/index.php?option=com_content&task=view&id=10213&Itemid=143.

8. "Iraq: millions at risk from polluted water," International Committee of the Red Cross, news release 08/196 (October 29, 2008).

9. The US-run Alhurra TV (November 6, 2007) (in Arabic).

10. Campbell Robertson, "Iraq private sector falters; rolls of government soar," *International Herald Tribune* (August 11, 2008).

11. According to Transparency International's 2008 Corruption Perceptions Index (CPI), which highlights the link between poverty, failed institutions, and graft. Published September 23, 2008.

12. "Many were displaced prior to 2003, but the largest number has fled since. In 2006, Iraqis became the leading nationality seeking asylum in Europe." See "The Continuing Needs of Iraq's Displaced," http://www.unhcr.org/iraq.html.

13. Ibid.

14. Including the International Organization for Migration (IOM) report (November 1, 2008), and a Washington-based international aid organization report (October 30, 2008).

15. "IRAQ: NGOs warn against encouraging large-scale refugee returns," Integrated Regional Information Networks (November 3, 2008).

16. There are 17,700 security detainees under US forces control, kept mainly between Camps Bucca in the south and Cropper near Baghdad, according to Task Force 134 (TF-134), which operates US detention facilities in Iraq. See Nick Mottern and Bill Rau, "Detention Has a Wide, Destructive Impact in Iraq," *TruthOut* (October 12 2008), http://www.truthout.org/101208C.

17. "Iraqi MP to UN: Investigate Iraq's Secret Prisons," Middle East Online (October 31, 2008).

18. Ibid. The ICRC said it has not yet reached an agreement with the Iraqi government on visiting prisons under their control.

19. "Iraq: No let-up in humanitarian crisis," International Committee of the Red Cross (March 15, 2008), http://www.icrc.org/web/eng/siteeng0.nsf/htmlall/iraq-report-170308/$file/ICRC-Iraq-report-0308-eng.pdf.

20. "MNF arrest women instead of their wanted relatives–MP," Voices of Iraq (November 1, 2008).

21. "Minister of women affairs reveals the suffering of Iraqi women detainees," Al Jazeera (January 25, 2009), http://www.aljazeera.net/NR/exeres/FF8F0DB9-A939-4480-AE0B-0997B03378EB.htm (in Arabic).

22. http://www.niqash.org/content.php?contentTypeID=74&id=2048&lang=0.

23. Patrick Cockburn, "Iraq allows doctors to carry guns for security," Independent (October 17, 2008).

24. These demands and principles have been issued, time and again, by various resistance groups since 2003. They have also been formulated by some international peace organizations in the last two years. See Justice for Iraq at http://www.justiceforiraq.blogspot.com/, http://www.aljazeera.net/news/archive/archive?ArchiveId=1095696 (in Arabic), and http://www.transnational.org/Area_MiddleEast/2007/TFF_Iraq_Peace_Plan.html.

INTRODUCTION

1. http://www.defenddemocracy.org/about_FDD/about_FDD_show.htm?doc_id=257042 &attrib_id=7615 (accessed October 2004; site now discontinued).

2. As Kan'an Makiya, head of the Iraqi Documentation and Studies Center, Harvard University, and professor at Brandeis University, told President Bush in a meeting at the White House. See "Bush Discusses Plans For Iraq," Middle East Economic Survey 46, no. 6(February 10, 2003),. http://www.mees.com/postedarticles/politics/ArabPressReview/a46n06c02.htm.

3. The Arabs of the peninsula have used the word "Iraq" for lands adjacent to water, including large rivers. The Persians conversely used a similar word for the lowlands or coastlands. Well-known archaeologists point out the Sumerian linguistic origin of "Uruk," which means "settlement." Uruk was also the name of one of the largest cities of ancient times (thirty kilometers away from southern city of Simawa in today's Iraq). In attested writings, the first mention of the name was in the twelfth century BC, in a Kish document that named the region ruled by Babylon as Eriqa, and it became widely used in the fourth and fifth centuries AD during the Sassanid (Persian) dynasty and in pre-Islamic poetry. All these are distinct from the use of the word "Mesopotemia" by the Greeks, ambiguous since it may apply to any two rivers in the region. See Taha Baqir, introduction to History of Ancient Civilizations: Summary of the History of Valley of the Two Rivers, Volume One, 2nd ed., by the Cultural Affairs Department, Ministry of Culture and Media (1985), 10.

4. A title given to women whose parents are noble descendants of Prophet Muhammad. The linguistic origin of the title is from Ali, the Prophet's cousin who married Fatima al-Zahra', the Prophet's only daughter to have children, giving birth to Hassan in 625 AD and Hussain in 626 AD. As the Prophet had no sons, they were loved dearly by the prophet, who treated them as if they were his sons. Therefore, their male descendents carry the noble religious title Sayid and the female descendents carry the noble title Alwiya.

5. "Updated Iraq Survey Affirms Earlier Mortality Estimates," Johns Hopkins Bloomberg School of Public Health and al-Mustansiriya University in Baghdad (October 11, 2006).

6. International Committee of the Red Cross, "Civilians without protection: The ever-worsening humanitarian crisis in Iraq," April 11, 2007, http://www.reliefweb.int/rw/RWFiles2007.nsf/FilesByRWDocUnidFilename/486FDBB72255800CC12572BA0029A8F4-Full_Report.pdf/$File/Full_Report.pdf.

7. United Nations Children's Fund (UNICEF) Security Council presentation, May 22, 2003, http://www.unicef.org/media/media_9109.html.

1. Ottoman rule continued to rely for its legitimacy on Islamic caliphates as the only way to maintain Islamic unity. This meant adherence to the principles of the first four Islamic caliphs, which followed Muhammad in Media in the seventh century A.D., including the obligation to protect the rights of the Christians, Jews, Sabaeans, and other monotheistic faiths.

2. The Iraqi poet, Jamil Sidqi al-Zahawi (1863–1936), conveyed the pain: "When ruin overtakes that land upon whose soil / You grew up, and you sorrow not, you are a stone."

3. The proclamation was issued to the inhabitants of Baghdad on March 19, 1917, by Lieutenant General Sir Stanley Maude. http://www.harpers.org/ProclamationBaghdad.html.

4. Robert Fisk, "Iraq, 1917," *Independent*, June 17, 2004.

5. See "Winston Churchill's Secret Poison Gas Memo," http://www.globalresearch.ca/articles/ CHU407A.html, which cites Companion Volume 4, Part 1 of the official biography by Martin Gilbert, *Winston S. Churchill*, (London: Heinemann, 1976).

6. T. E. Lawrence, "A Report on Mesopotamia," *Sunday Times*, August 22, 1920, http://www.globalpolicy.org/security/issues/iraq/history/1920arabia.htm.

7. Gertrude Bell, "The Letters [21 August 1921]," *The Gertrude Bell Archive*, http://www.gerty.ncl.ac.uk/ letters/l1447.htm.

8. On August 21, 1921, Gertrude Bell, Oriental secretary to the high commissioner, wrote to her father about the transfer of sovereignty to Iraqis: "Muzahim Pachachi (the one who made the speech in English at our tea party at Basra) and another barrister whom you don't know, Rauf Beg Chadirji, a pal of mine, and still more splendid was one of the shaikhs of the northern shammar, Ajil al-Yawar; I had seen him in 1917 when he came in to us." In a July 20, 1921, letter to her father, she referred to "Saiyid Muhammad Sadr . . . a tall black-bearded *alim* [cleric] with a sinister expression. . . . We tried to arrest him early in August but failed. He escaped from Baghdad and moved about the country like a flame of war, rousing the tribes." The grandsons of Pachachi, Chadirji, and Yawar were members of Bremer's interim Governing Council, while the grandson of Sadr led a populist anti-occupation movement and also avoided arrest.

9. Roger D. Hodge, "Weekly Review," *Harper's*, January 27, 2004, http://www.harpers.org/WeeklyReview2004-01-27.html#20040126-150584459206.

10. Worn by both men and women. While men have the abaya on their shoulders, women cover their hair.

11. Ferial Ghazoul, "Iraqi woman as a literary figure in the 20th century," in *Encyclopaedia of Arab Women Writers* 3 (2004), 10. (In Arabic.)

12. Ahmed Fayadh al-Mafriji, *Women in Modern Iraqi Poetry* (Baghdad: University Press, 1958). (In Arabic.)

13. Al-Zahawi was from a religious Kurdish family settled in Baghdad; his father was the Mufti of Baghdad.

14. Hanna Batatu, *The Old Social Classes and the Revolutionary Movements of Iraq* (Princeton, NJ: Princeton University Press, 1978), 393.

15. The first Alliance School for Jewish boys was established in Baghdad in December 1864 with forty-three pupils, while the first Alliance School for Jewish girls was opened in 1893. See Fadhel al-Barak, *Iranian and Jewish Schools in Iraq*, 2nd ed. (Baghdad: Al dar Arabiya, 1985), 29. (In Arabic.)

16. In 1914, there were 600 girls and 378 boys in public schools, 2,663 girls and 8,020 boys in private, religious, and foreign schools. See Wamidh Omar Nadhmi, *1920: Political, Ideological and Social Roots of Arab Nationalist Movement in Iraq*, 2nd ed. (Baghdad: Center for Arab Unity Studies, 1985), 85. (In Arabic.)

17. Including Asma al-Zahawi (al-Zahawi's sister), Nouma Sultan Hamouda, Hassiba Jaafar, Paulina Hassoun. and wives of Prime Minister Nouri al-Saeed and Jaffar al-Askari. It faced protests from conservatives, especially after publishing *Layla*, a journal promoting education and employment rights for women.

18. Sami Rafael Bati, *Iraqi Journalism, Rafael Bati's Writings*, vol. 1 (Baghdad: Al-Adib, 1985). (In Arabic.)

19. Among the contributors were famous poets and journalists such as al-Zahawi, al-Rusafi, Selma Saiegh, Yousif Ghanema, and Anwer Soul.

20. Shooting at demonstrators by the police took place in 1936, 1941, and 1948. See Hanna Batatu, *The Old Social Classes and the Revolutionary Movements of Iraq* (Princeton, NJ: Princeton University Press, 1978), 545–557, and 467, for table of uprisings, coups, and revolutions in Iraq since the British occupation.

21. In 1949, after the suppression of al-Wathbah, Fahd, the leader and founder of the Communist Party, and two Political Bureau members were executed in public.

22. Hanna Batatu, *The Old Social Classes and the Revolutionary Movements of Iraq* (Princeton, NJ: Princeton University Press, 1978), 30, 34.

23. The number of state college students increased from 99 in 1921–22, to 1,218 in 1940–41, to 8,568 in 1958–59, and the number of state secondary school students grew from 229, to 13,969, to 73,911 in the same years. See Layla Zaidan, *Women Solve Their Problems* (Baghdad: League for the Defense of Women's Rights, 1958), 29. (In Arabic.)

24. Ibid.

25. Hanna Batatu, *The Old Social Classes and the Revolutionary Movements of Iraq* (Princeton, NJ: Princeton University Press, 1978), 34.

26. Aminah ar-Rahhal was a law student who lived in Baghdad, in an area where the majority were Christians and Jews. Like them she started wearing a long coat and a hat. Her brother Husain ar-Rahhal encouraged her to buy a car and drive in Baghdad, a rare act, except among European women. See Saniha Amin Zaki, *Memoir of an Iraqi Woman Doctor* (London: Dar al-Hikma, 2005), 172. (In Arabic.)

27. Ali al-Wardi, *Social Aspects of Iraqi Modern History* (Baghdad, 1977).

28. Among its members were Naziha al-Dilami, Rose Khadduri, Victoria Nouman, Afifa al-Bustani, Aminah ar-Rahhal, and Nadhima Wahbi, most of these members of the Communist Party.

29. Souad Khairy, *Iraqi Women's Struggle and Offerings* (Stockholm: All-Tryck, 1998), 6. (In Arabic.)

30. Twenty-nine Asian and African countries representing over half the world's population, most of which were newly independent, sent delegates to this conference in Bandung, Indonesia, April 18–24, 1955. The conference was organized by Egypt, Indonesia, Burma, Ceylon (Sri Lanka), India, and Pakistan, with the stated aims to promote Afro-Asian economic and cultural cooperation, and to oppose colonialism and neocolonialism by the United States, the Soviet Union, and any other imperialistic nation. Chinese prime minister Zhou Enlai attended to quiet fears of some anticommunist delegates concerning China's intentions. A ten-point "declaration on promotion of world peace and cooperation," incorporating the principles of the United Nations Charter and Jawaharal Nehru's principles was adopted unanimously.

31. Edith and E. F. Penrose, *Iraq: International Relations and National Development* (Boulder, CO: Westview Press, 1978), 214.

32. Shakir Hanish, "The July 14th 1958 Revolution in Iraq," http://www.iraqcp.org/0030711shE .htm.

33. Ibid.

34. Nazik led a secluded life in Egypt until her death in June 2007; Lamiah lives in the United States.

35. M. Badawi, *An Anthology of Modern Arabic Verse* (Oxford: Oxford University Press, 1970), 18.

36. Nazik al-Malaika, *Modern Poetry in Translation* 19 (2003). "Iraqi Poetry Today," guest editor, Saadi Simawe.

37. Translated by Sara Marsden, *Ur* 2/3 (1982), 136.

38. Baghdad is divided into two parts by the Tigris River that flows through the center of the city; the eastern part called al-Karkh and the western part al-Risafa. The fortified Green Zone where Bremer resided for a year is in al-Karkh.

39. Ahmed Hassan al-Bakr led the second Ba'ath coup in 1968 with Saddam Hussein as lieutenant, while Ali Saleh al-Sa'di later broke with the Ba'ath party in 1964, citing its link to the CIA, and formed another radical Arab nationalist party in exile.

40. K. Aburish, who worked with Saddam in the 1970s, has said that the CIA's role in the coup against Qasim was "substantial," and that "the relationship between the Americans and the Ba'ath Party at that moment in time was very close indeed." To get rid of Qasim, the "terrorist" label of the fifties and sixties (i.e., "communist") was useful as a cover to justify establishing contacts with the exiled Ba'ath leaders. "The plans to overthrow the Iraqi leader, led by William Lakeland who was stationed at the Baghdad embassy as an attaché, represented one of the most elaborate CIA operations in the history of the Middle East," said K. Aburish, *Saddam Hussein: The Politics of Revenge* (London: Bloomsbury, 2001), 55.

41. The Ba'athist ideology combines elements of Arab nationalism, anti-imperialism and socialism. Saddam Hussein joined the party in 1957, and remained loyal to its ideas throughout his life.

42. Sa'ad Jawad, *Iraq and the Kurdish Question 1958–1970* (London: Ithaca Press, 1981), 227.

43. Saddam had until 1979 shared power for eleven years with General Ahmed Hassan al-Bakr, a military Ba'athist, as his deputy, and with a Ba'ath party leadership that had a few centers of power and complex dynamics. It has become common for friends and foes of the Ba'ath era to treat it as a single thirty-five-year rule by Saddam.

44. Karim El-Gawhary, "The right to reintegrate," *Al-Ahram Weekly On-line*, July 29, 2004, http://weekly.ahram.org.eg/2004/701/re84.htm.

45. "De-Ba'athification committee purges Iraqi universities of publications of the Ba'ath regime," *Aasharq al-Awsat*, January 4, 2006. (In Arabic.)

46. Yousif Salman Yousif was born in Baghdad in 1901. He was known internationally as Fahad. He was publicly hanged with members of the ICP politburo by the monarchy on February 14, 1949, following the ICP strike for higher wages at Haditha Petroleum pumping station, a strike that had culminated in a march on Baghdad in 1948.

47. Hamid Majid Moussa, the general secretary of the ICP, was selected as a member of the Governing Council for being of Shi'a origin, in accordance with the strict sectarian and ethnic quota system imposed by Paul Bremer.

48. The 5th Conference of the Iraqi Women's League (IWL) was held in Baghdad on July 24–25, 2005, under the slogan, "A Peaceful and Democratic Iraq is the Guarantee for Women's Equality and Children's Happiness." It was attended by ninety-eight delegates, none of whom addressed the occupation. http://www.iraqiwomenleague.org/women-conf-2006.html.

49. "Writings of comrade Fahad, on March 8, international women's day," *Al Qa'eda*, August 9–11, 1944. Translated from Arabic by Peter Philips.

50. Ibid.

51. On June 1, 1972, a state-owned company, the Iraqi Company for Oil Operations (ICOO), was established to take over IPC facilities. By 1975, all remaining foreign interests were nationalized.

52. Helen Chapin Metz, ed., *Iraq: A Country Study* (Washington, DC: GPO for the Library of Congress, 1988), http://countrystudies.us/iraq.

53. S. al-Khayat. *The Position of Iraqi Women within the Family: With Particular Reference to Married Women* (PhD diss., University of Keele, 1985), 85.

54. The Iraqi Bureau of Statistics reported that in 1976, women constituted approximately 38.5 percent of those in the education profession, 31 percent of the medical profession, 25 percent of lab technicians, 15 percent of accountants, and 15 percent of civil servants. See Human Rights Watch, *Background on Women's Status in Iraq Prior to the Fall of the Saddam Hussein Government*, briefing paper, November 2003.

55. G. R. Popal, "Impact of sanctions on the population of Iraq." *Eastern Mediterranean Health Journal* 6, no.4 (July 2000), 791–95.

56. Including Aziz el-Haj, the general secretary, who appeared on Iraqi TV calling for all political opponents to follow the Ba'ath. He was rewarded by the regime, which appointed him as Iraq's ambassador to United Nations Educational, Scientific and Cultural Organization (UNESCO) in Paris, and would later side with the US-led invasion of Iraq.

57. Mundher al-Adhami, an Iraqi academic, had met Khalid briefly in London in 1965: "Despair about the ICP was growing among us along with recognizing the sterility of the Soviet experiment. That brief meeting in London revived my hopes for revolutionary ideals and even for the ICP itself. Khalid with his intellect, energy, and modesty exuded strength, optimism and commitment."

58. Not much has been written about the CL activity in exile, even though some of the members are now elderly, necessitating a record of their testimonies. Mundher, who had moved to London in the late sixties to continue his studies, writes with an eye to the legacy of Khalid: "In a quickly curtailed visit to Iraq late in 1968, I met old friends who were working with Khalid, including Rafi' al-Kubaisi and Sami Mohammed Ali. They soon fell in the struggle, Rafi' in armed confrontation in the Marshes, and Sami under torture in Qasr al-Nihaya prison. That must have been the spur for me to re-engage with the left-wing politics. We formed a Committee for the Defense of the Iraqi People, working with Russell Foundation in London, which led to my Iraqi passport being withdrawn by the Iraqi embassy. The name of the committee and the link with the foundation are a continuation of Khalid's work following the Ba'ath coup of 1963. A loose group formed within the Iraqi Student Association in the 70s, opposing the line of the leadership of the ICP collaborating with the Ba'ath. We constituted ourselves in the Iraqi Revolutionary Grouping as enlightened revolutionary Marxists and produced a periodical entitled *Al Naseer'* [Partisan] using pen-names. The 13 issues of the magazine, which I edited with the architect Talaat al-Banna, apparently did have some intellectual influence, and a few of their articles were republished in Arabic newspapers like *al-Raya* in Beirut. We forged links with Palestinian groups, then gradually attached ourselves to a remaining group of Khalid's organization, headed by Ibrahim Allawi and continuing armed struggle. This is the same group that Haifa Zangana joined in Baghdad and Kurdistan. Abroad, and away from maneuvering with Syrian and Kurdish contacts by the leaders, we pressed for a wider left-democratic front to oppose the Ba'ath regime. The link with the reminder of the CL proved with time a great disappointment, a mark of our naivety." Private correspondence, March 17, 2007.

59. An independent group of intellectuals in Britain that was formed around the magazine *al-Naseer* (Partisan), supporting the revolutionary struggle in Iraq, had by that time attached themselves to some of the cadres that survived the purges and massacres but disintegrated in the 1980s.

60. Amina Haider al-Sadr, (1938–80), also called Bint-al-Huda, was in her twenties when she began writing articles in *al-Adhwa*, the Islamic magazine printed by the religious intellectuals of al-Najaf, Iraq, in 1959. She was also a novelist. In 1980, she was executed. She was a cousin of the religious leader Muqtada al-Sadr.

61. Souad Khayat, *Iraqi Women's Struggle and Offerings* (Stockholm: All-Tryck, 1998), 123. (In Arabic.)

62. Joyce Battle, ed. *Shaking Hands with Saddam Hussein: The U.S. Tilts toward Iraq, 1980–1984*, National Security Archive Electronic Briefing Book No. 82, February 25, 2003, http://www.gwu.edu/~nsarchiv/NSAEBB/NSAEBB82.

63. Many of the manual jobs, including ones in agriculture, were carried out by migrant Egyptian laborers, sometimes estimated at one million. More white-collar and professional positions were available to women.

64. Helen Chapin Metz, ed., "Paramilitary forces," in *Iraq: A Country Study*, (Washington, DC: GPO for the Library of Congress, 1988), http://countrystudies.us/iraq; http://countrystudies.us/iraq/95.htm.

65. Karim Hamza, "Evaluating the status of Iraqi women in light of the Beijing platform for action" (United Nations Development Fund for Women [UNIFEM], 2004), http://www.iknowpolitics.org/en/node/35.

66. Helen Chapin Metz, ed., "Iraq, education and welfare," in *Iraq: A Country Study* (Washington, DC: GPO for the Library of Congress, 1988), http://countrystudies.us/iraq/45.htm.

67. "Persian Gulf War: set up of Iraq," Iraq Resource Information Site, http://www.geocities.com/iraqinfo/gulfwar/setup.html.

68. The sanctions included a full trade embargo barring all imports from and exports to Iraq, excepting only medical supplies, foodstuffs, and other items of humanitarian need, as determined by the Security Council Sanctions Committee, which was also established by Resolution 661.

69. Denis Halliday, a former UN assistant secretary-general and, from September 1997 to September 1998, the UN humanitarian coordinator of the Oil-for-Food Programme, said that sanctions against Iraq amount to "genocide." Mark Siegal, "Former UN official says sanctions against Iraq amount to 'genocide'," *Cornell Chronicle*, September 30, 1999, http://www.news.cornell.edu/chronicle/99/9.30.99/Halliday_talk.html.

70. In May 1996, *60 Minutes* correspondent Lesley Stahl asked Madeleine Albright, US ambassador to the UN, "We have heard that half a million children have died [as a result of sanctions]. I mean, that is more children than died in Hiroshima. And, you know, is the price worth it?" Albright responded, "I think that is a very hard choice, but the price, we think, the price is worth it." The sanctions continued for nearly seven more years, up to the invasion of 2003.

71. According to the Center for Economic and Social Rights, "There had been a great deal of speculation outside Iraq that the ration system was used selectively as a reward and punishment device by the Iraqi regime against various sections of the population. The 1991 visit found no evidence for this. On the contrary, it was found that even people who were quite outspoken in their opposition to the regime received the ration and were satisfied with the functioning of the ration system." Peter Boone, Harris Gazdar, and Athar Hussain, *Sanctions Against Iraq: Costs of Failure*, Center for Economic and Social Rights, November 1997.

72. Karim Hamza, "Evaluating the status of Iraqi women in light of the Beijing platform for action," UNIFEM, 2004, http://www.iknowpolitics.org/en/node/35.

73. Souad N. al-Azzawi, "Depleted Uranium Radioactive Contamination In Iraq: An Overview," *Global Research*, August 31, 2006, http://www.globalresearch.ca/index.php?context=viewArticle&code=AL-20060831&articleId=3116.

74. Karim Hamza, "Evaluating the status of Iraqi women in light of the Beijing platform for action," UNIFEM, 2004, http://www.iknowpolitics.org/en/node/35.

75. Associated Press, "UNICEF: Sanctions Hurt Iraq Schools," December 10, 1998.

76. Tim Weiner, "U.S. Spied on Iraq Under U.N. Cover, Officials Now Say," *New York Times*, January 7, 1999, http://why-war.com/news/1999/01/07/usspiedo.html.

77. Michael Wolff, "The Students of Moustanserya University: How Sanctions Destroy Iraqi Education," *CounterPunch*, February 22, 2003, http://www.counterpunch.org/wolff02222003.html.

78. There has been a bitter conflict between Islamic and secular Arab nationalist and Left movements in the Arab world, exemplified in execution and suppression of Islamic groups in Egypt, Syria, and Iraq. In 1989, the Beirut-based Centre for Arab Unity Studies, headed by K. Haseab, convened a

seminar for pan-Arab religious dialogue, which resulted in a preparatory committee for the establishment of an Islamic (Arab) National Congress. This brought under one roof most of the intellectuals of the two trends, including Marxists and patriotic liberals.

79. For more details and thorough examination of the status of Iraqi women and the work of the GFIW, see Karim Hamza, "Evaluating the status of Iraqi women in light of the Beijing platform for action," UNIFEM, 2004, http://www.iknowpolitics.org/en/node/35.

80. Nabil al-Nawwab, "Report on the Consultative Mission to the General Federation of Iraqi Women: Project Proposal for the Development of the Women's Sector," United Nations Economic and Social Commission for Western Asia, 2000. (In Arabic.)

II. INVADING IRAQ

1. See Faiza al-Arji's account of her experience as an Iraqi women activist at a "democracy in Iraq" conference hosted by a few US organizations in Jordan. Faiza al-Arji, *A Family in Baghdad*, April 17, 2005, http://afamilyinbaghdad.blogspot.com/2005_04_17_afamilyinbagh dad_archive.html#111376172909912353.

2. US Department of State, "Human rights and women in Iraq: voices of Iraqi women," Foreign Press Center Briefing, March 6, 2003, http://www.state.gov/g/rls/rm/2003/18477.htm.

3. The following is the development of my work on US-funded Iraqi NGOs and women's organizations, part of which was titled "The Three Cyclops of Empire-building: Targeting the Fabric of Iraqi Society," published in *Empire's Law*, ed. Amy Bartholomew (Pluto Press, 2006) and "Colonial Feminists from Washington to Baghdad: Women for a Free Iraq as a Case Study," in *Barriers to Reconciliation*, ed. Jacqueline S. Ismael and William W. Haddad (University Press of America, 2006).

4. Secretary of State Colin L. Powell, Remarks to the National Foreign Policy Conference for Leaders of NGOs, Washington, DC, October 26, 2001.

5. Andrew Natsios, Speaking on the last day of Interaction's three-day forum, June 9, 2003.

6. Abby Stoddard, "With Us or Against Us? NGO Neutrality on the Line," *Global Policy Forum* (December 2003), http://www.globalpolicy.org/ngos/fund/2003/1200against.htm.

7. According to the group's 2002 IRS Form 990, Free Iraq Foundation, Inc., received $1.66 million in support for 2001, 99.97 percent of that figure coming from public funding sources. In 2000, the group's income was $1 million; for 1998 and 1999, $265,000 and $580,000 respectively. "Iraq Foundation," *SourceWatch*, http://www.sourcewatch.org/ index.php?title=Iraq_Foundation.

8. Allawi is the head of the Iraqi National Accord, an exile organization dedicated to the overthrow of Saddam. The group had been under CIA patronage since 1992. Jon Lee Anderson, "A Man of the Shadows: Can Iyad Allawi Hold Iraq Together?" *New Yorker*, January 24, 2005, http://www.newyorker.com/archive/2005/01/24/050124fa_fact1.

9. L. Paul Bremer and Malcolm McConnell, *My Year in Iraq: The Struggle to Build a Future of Hope* (New York: Simon & Schuster, 2006), 385.

10. Ibid. Judy Van Rest is one of the Coalition Provisional Authority's political officers.

11. US Department of State, "U.S. Commitment to Women in Iraq," Office of the Senior Coordinator for International Women's Issues, June 22, 2005, http://www.state.gov/g/wi/rls/ 48464.htm.

12. Lindsey Brooks, "Iraqi Women Speak Out about Life under Saddam's Dictatorship, October 4, 2002," Washington File, October 9, 2002, http://www.usembassy.it/file2002_10/alia/a2100906 .htm.

13. The women's organization of the Communist Party, which was licensed to work publicly during the establishment of the National Progressive Front, consisting of the dominant Ba'ath Party and the Communist Parties of 1973–79.

14. Jane Ciabattari, "Survivor of Attacks Speaks for Iraqi Women," *Women's eNews*, December 10, 2002, http://www.womensenews.org/article.cfm/dyn/aid/1140/context/archive.

15. Ibid. Michael continued to lament the misfortune of women, saying, "The opposition leaders are meeting today in London with the U.S. State Department to discuss the future of Iraq, post-Saddam Hussein. There are no Iraqi women among the opposition leaders expected there."

16. Jeevan Vasagar and Brian Whitaker, "Exiles Cited by PM are Backed by Iran," *Guardian*, February 19, 2003, http://politics.guardian.co.uk/foreignaffairs/story/0,,898354,00.html.

17. "Women for a Free Iraq Campaign," Foundation for Defense of Democracies, http://www.defenddemocracy.org/programs/programs_show.htm?doc_id=192125&attrib_id=100 14.

18. See my essay, "Colonial Feminists from Washington to Baghdad: Women for a Free Iraq as a Case Study," in *Barriers to Reconciliation*, ed. Jacqueline S. Ismael and William W. Haddad (University Press of America, 2006).

19. On the same day, Tony Blair read a succession of letters and e-mails from Iraqi exiles as proof that a war to remove Saddam was supported by Iraqis. Jeevan Vasagar and Brian Whitaker, "Exiles Cited by PM are Backed by Iran," *Guardian*, February 19, 2003, http://politics.guardian.co.uk/foreignaffairs/story/0,,898354,00.html.

20. FDD is a think tank that claims to conduct "research and education on international terrorism—the most serious security threat to the United States and other free, democratic nations." According to Jeffrey Blankfort, a Jewish, anti-Zionist activist in California (former editor of the *Middle East Labor Review*), the FDD "is one of the most influential and powerful of the Zionist lobbies which changed its name and sprung into action immediately after 9-11." Its board of directors has included Steve Forbes, Jack Kemp, and Jeanne Kirkpatrick. Newt Gingrich, James Woolsey, Richard Perle, and Bill Kristol have served as advisers. See "Foundation for the Defense of Democracies," *SourceWatch*, http://www.sourcewatch.org/index.php?title=Foundation_for_the_Defense_of_Democracies. 20. Randy Scheunemann, a former Rumsfeld advisor who helped draft the Iraq Liberation Act of 1998, authorizing $98 million in US aid to Iraqi exile groups, was the founding president of the Committee for the Liberation of Iraq. Now he's helping former Soviet-bloc states win business there. "War profiteering," *SourceWatch*, http://www.sourcewatch.org/index.php?title=War_profiteering.

21. US Department of State, "Iraqi Women Under Saddam's Regime: A Population Silenced," Office of International Women's Issues, March 20, 2003, http://www.state.gov/g/wi/rls/18877.htm.

22. For profiles of the thirty Iraqi "women leaders," according to the Independent Women's Forum, see Independent Women's Forum, "A Quest for Political, Economic and Social Participation in a Democratic Iraq," August 16, 2004, http://www.iwf.org/iraq/iraq_detail.asp?ArticleID=625, and Nick Schou, "Going to Bed with a $3000,000 Price on Your Head," *OC Weekly*, February 24, 2005, http://www.ocweekly.com/news/news/going-to-bed-with-a-300000-price-on-your-head/19098/.

23. Ibid.

24. Foundation for the Defense of Democracies, "Success stories," http://www.defenddemocracy.org/about_FDD/about_FDD_show.htm?doc_id=257042&attri_id=7615.

25. According to the FDD Web site, the campaign's media placements were estimated to have reached over fifty million Americans.

26. Women's Alliance for a Democratic Iraq, "Background History," http://www.wafdi.org/background.

27. The group remained active under occupation, with three members serving as ministers in the interim government (Nasreen Barwari, Mishkat el-Mounim, and Pascale Warda), and another serving as Iraq's representative to the United States (Rend al-Rahim Francke).

28. Women's Alliance for a Democratic Iraq, "US-Iraqi Business Sorority Program," http://www.wafdi.org/projects.

29. Ms. Ala Talabani, a member of the Patriotic Union of Kurdistan Party, for example, was a cofounder of WFFI, then of the Iraqi Women's High Council in October 2003, then of the Iraqi Women's Network in 2004. Rend al-Rahim Francke, the executive director of the Iraq Foundation, moved on to cofound WFFI. Tanya Gilly, manager of the Democracy Programs at the FDD, is a founding member of WFFI and WAFDI. Zainab al-Suwaij, Safiya Taleb al-Suhail, and others, are active in more than three NGOs at a time.

30. "The Iraqi women were joined in the Oval Office by American soldiers that had just returned from Iraq. They were eager to thank the soldiers for their freedom and for their personal sacrifice on behalf of the Iraqi people," said Raz Rasool, the executive director of WAFDI. She characterized her meeting with the president by saying, "We have met the brave soldiers, American soldiers."

31. Foundation for the Defense of Democracies, "Promoting Democracy Activists," http://www.defenddemocracy.org/programs/programs_show.htm?doc_id=308432&attrib_id=100 14.

32. http://www.georgiabizupdate.com/pdf/white-house-women-0408.pdf (site discontinued).

33. Foundation for the Defense of Democracies, "About the Foundation," http://www.defenddemocracy.org/about_fdd/about_fdd_list.htm?attrib_id=7615.

34. Letter to Paul Bremer from WAFDI and its affiliated group, the WFFI, January 23, 2004, in which they demanded that the United States should address the growing threat to women's rights and religious freedom posed by Islamist parties and clerics who seek to establish Islamic rule in Iraq more aggressively. "We fear that the United States will fail in the forward strategy of freedom in the greater Middle East that is a cornerstone of President Bush's presidency."

35. Jim Lobe, "Politics-US: Foe of 'Radical Feminism' to Train Iraqi Women," Inter Press Service, October 5, 2004.

36. Formed to protest language in the draft constitution that makes Islam the sole source for Iraqi law.

37. The Iraqi Women's Educational Institute, a joint project of the American Islamic Congress, the Foundation for the Defense of Democracies, and the Independent Women's Forum, was also present. Independent Women's Forum, "Iraqi Women Fighting to Save Rights in Draft Constitution," August 3, 2005, http://www.iwf.org/iraq/iraq_detail.asp?ArticleID=792.

38. Spirit of America, "Join Us and Make Freedom Win," http://www.spiritofamerica.net/site.

39. Daniel Henninger, "Wonder Land: Spirit of America: Here's a Way You Can Help the Cause in Iraq," OpinionJournal, April 16, 2004, http://www.opinionjournal.com/columnists/dhenninger/?id=110004958.

40. "Whether in the hands of patriarchal men or feminists," writes Harvard professor Leila Ahmed, "the ideas of western feminism essentially functioned to morally justify the attack on native societies and to support the notion of comprehensive superiority of [the United States and] Europe." Ghali Hassan, "Colonial Violence Against Women in Iraq," Countercurrents.org, May 31, 2004, http://www.countercurrents.org/iraq-hassan310504.htm.

41. Security Council Resolution 1325 was passed unanimously on October 31, 2000. It specifically addresses the impact of war on women, and women's contributions to conflict resolution and sustainable peace.

42. Dr. Raja al-Khuzai was one of the US administration's favorites. In one of his speeches, Bush said, "I want to thank my friend, Dr. Raja Khuzai, who's with us today. This is the third time we have met. The first time we met, she walked into the Oval Office . . . the door opened up. She said, 'My liberator,' and burst out in tears—(laughter)—and so did I. (Applause.)" White House Office of the Press Secretary, "President, Mrs. Bush Mark Progress in Global Women's Human Rights," press release, March 12, 2004, http://www.whitehouse.gov/ news/releases/2004/03/20040312-5.html.

43. The provisional government of Iraq from July 13, 2003, to June 1, 2004, was established by and served under the US-led Coalition Provisional Authority. The Council's ethnic and religious breakdown included thirteen Shi'ites, five Sunni Arabs, five Kurds (also Sunnis), one ethnic Turk, and an Assyrian Christian.

44. They are Narmin Othman (Environment), Bayan Dizayi (Housing & Construction), Wijdan Michael (Human Rights), and Faten Mahmoud (Women's Affairs).

45. http://www.washtimes.com/national/20050203-125019-2769r.htm (site discontinued).

46. *Remember Fallujah*, http://www.rememberfallujah.org.

47. Peter Popham, "US Forces 'Used Chemical Weapons' During Assault on City of Fallujah," *Independent*, November 8, 2005, http://news.independent.co.uk/world/middle_east/article325560.ece.

48. Dahr Jamail, "Stories from Fallujah," *Dahr Jamail's Weblog*, February 8, 2005, http://dahrjamailiraq.com/weblog/archives/dispatches/000196.php.

49. See "Fallujah Death Toll for Week More Than 600," *USA Today*, April 11, 2004, http://www.usatoday.com/news/world/iraq/2004-04-11-fallujah-casualties_x.htm.

50. "U.S. Probes Shooting at Fallujah Mosque: Video Shows Marine Killing Wounded Iraqi, MSNBC, November 16, 2004, http://www.msnbc.msn.com/id/6496898.

51. *Remember Fallujah*, http://www.rememberfallujah.org.

52. Edward Said, "The Arab Condition," *Al-Ahram Weekly*, May 22, 2003.

53. Noah Feldman, "The Way We Live Now: 7-31-05; Foundering?" *New York Times Magazine*, July 31, 2004.

54. WAFDI is represented today by six members in the National Assembly (out of 70 women and 275 total representatives).

55. Ninety-five percent of Iraqis are Muslims. The rest are Christians and Yazidis.

56. Surah 24: Ayah 31.

57. Literally "hijab" means "veil," "curtain," "partition," or "separation."

58. Sana Ayoub Sabri al-Khayyat, "The Position of Iraqi Women within the Family: With Particular Reference to Married Women" (PhD diss., University of Keele, 1985).

III. LIFE UNDER OCCUPATION

1. "Kurdish Youth Have Lost Trust in KRG," *Kurdish Aspect*, January 15, 200,. http://www.kurdishaspect.com/doc0115KA.html.

2. E-mail from Shaista Aziz, February 27, 2007.

3. Integrated Regional Information Networks, "Iraqi Widow Numbers Rise in Wake of Violence," *DemocracyRising.us*, April 28, 2006, http://democracyrising.us/content/view/477/164.

4. Amnesty International, "Iraq: Decades of Suffering, Now Women Deserve Better," February 22, 2005, http://web.amnesty.org/library/Index/ENGMDE140012005.

5. United Nations High Commissioner for Refugees (UNHCR) spokeswoman Astrid van Gen-deren Stort said there were around 34,000 Palestinians in Iraq in 2003, and around 15,000 remain. See Ammar Alwan, "Palestinian refugees in Iraq stuck in 'Catch 22'," Mar 16, 2007, http://www.alertnet.org/thenews/newsdesk/ PAR646035.htm.

6. Including Ali and Hamza Shihab, young sons of Haleema Shihab; Muhammad, husband of Haleema Shihab; Hussein al-Ali, one of the most popular singers in western Iraq; Fatima Ma'athi, twenty-five, and her two young sons, Raad, four, and Raed, six; Simoya, the wife of Haji Rakat, and her two daughters; and Hamda Suleman. See http://debatebothsides.com/archive/index.php/ t-25593.html.

7. Rory McCarthy, "'U.S. Soldiers Started to Shoot Us One by One,'" Guardian, May 21, 2004, http://www.guardian.co.uk/Iraq/Story/0,2763,1221658,00.html. "Alongside her in the ward yes-terday were three badly injured girls from the Rakat family: Khalood Mohammed, aged just a year and struggling for breath, Moaza Rakat, twelve, and Iqbal Rakat, fifteen, whose right foot doctors had already amputated."

8. Ibid.

9. Ellen Knickmeyer, "In Haditha, Memories of a Massacre," Washington Post, May 27, 2006, http://www.washingtonpost.com/wp-dyn/content/article/2006/05/26/AR2006052602069.html.

10. Martin Asser, "What happened at Haditha?" BBC News, December 21, 2006, http://news.bbc.co.uk/1/hi/world/middle_east/5033648.stm.

11. The BBC uncovered video evidence that challenged the US military's account of events that took place in the town of Ishaqi in March. British Broadcasting Corporation, "New 'Iraq Massacre' Tape Emerges," June 2, 2006, http://news.bbc.co.uk/1/hi/world/middle_east/5039420.stm.

12. Ibid.

13. Associated Press, "Iraq-Day: Deadly Incidents Reported Tuesday," International Herald Tribune, November 14, 2006, http://www.iht.com/articles/ap/2006/11/15/africa/ME_GEN_Iraq _Day.php.

14. There are 44,000 private security contractors in Iraq, forming what the US Senate dubbed the "largest private army in the world." About 21,000 of those private guards are British—approxi-mately three times the total number of British troops in the country. There are also large numbers of North Americans, South Africans, Zimbabweans, and Gurkhas. See Kim Sengupta, "Security Staff Who Make up a Private Army in Iraq," Independent, May 30, 2007, http://news.independent.co .uk/world/middle_east/article2594165.ece. On death squads, see Michael Hirsh and John Barry, "The Salvador Option: The Pentagon May Put Special-Forces-led Assassination or Kidnapping Teams in Iraq," Newsweek, January 14, 2005.

15. http://www.freep.com/apps/pbcs.dll/article?AID=/20061113/NEWS07/611130351/1009/ NEWS07 (site discontinued).

16. BRussells Tribunal, "Iraqi Media Professionals Killed in Iraq under US Occupation," http://www.brusselstribunal.org/Journalists.htm.

17. Middle East Studies Association, "Professors' Associations Decry Violence Against Academic Colleagues in Iraq," MESA, July 5, 2006, http://mesa.wns.ccit.arizona.edu/ about/statements.htm#IraqJuly2006.

18. http://news.yahoo.com/s/afp/20061028/wl_mideast_afp/iraqunrestwomen_061028112402 (site discontinued).

19. Ibid.

20. Reporters Without Borders, "Journalists Fall Victim to Ethnic and Sectarian Violence, US Troops Carry out More Unlawful Arrests," October 31, 2006, http://www.rsf.org/article .php3?id_article=19497.

21. She was freed two days later after being interrogated at length about her links with armed groups. Her response was that it was her job as a journalist to maintain contacts with many kinds of people, including members of the military, Iraqi police officers, and members of resistance groups. She was re-arrested within a week and provisionally released after being held illegally for a month by Iraqi security authorities. Reporters Without Borders, "Tikrit-based Reporter Released Provisionally, Banned from Leaving Country," October 18, 2006, http://iraktribunal.de/aktiv/gulshan _all-bayati_rwb_on_release.html.

22. Amnesty International, "Middle East and North Africa: Iraq," *Amnesty International Report*, 2006, http://web.amnesty.org/report2006/irq-summary-eng.

23. United Nations Assistance Mission for Iraq (UNAMI), *Human Rights Report*, November 1–December 31, 2006, http://www.uniraq.org/FileLib/misc/HR%20Report%20Nov%20Dec%202006%20EN .pdf.

24. Mohammed Salih, "Bloody Years for Journalists in Iraq," *Antiwar.com* (from Inter Press Service), January 3, 2007, http://www.antiwar.com/ips/salih.php?articleid=10257.

25. Hugh Macleod, "Despair of Baghdad turns into a life of shame in Damascus," *Guardian*, October 24, 2006, quoting a UNHCR report.

26. United Nations Assistance Mission for Iraq (UNAMI), *Human Rights Report*, November 1–December 31, 2006, http://www.uniraq.org/FileLib/misc/HR%20Report%20Nov%20Dec%202006%20EN .pdf.

27. Peter Beaumont, "Hidden Victims of a Brutal Conflict: Iraq's Women," *Observer*, October 8, 2006, http://observer.guardian.co.uk/world/story/0,,1890260,00.html, quoting Aida Ussayran, former deputy human rights minister and now one of the women on the Council of Representatives.

28. Akeel Hussein and Colin Freeman, "Two Dead Soldiers, Eight More to Go, Vow Avengers of Iraqi Girl's Rape," *Telegraph*, October 7, 2006, http://www.telegraph.co.uk/news/main .jhtml?xml=/ news/2006/07/09/wirq09.xml.

29. Associated Press, "Soldier Gets 90 Years in Iraqi Rape Case," from MSNBC, November 17, 2006, http://www.msnbc.msn.com/id/15733192.

30. Yahoo! News, "U.S. Soldier Gets 100 years in Prison for Rape, Murder of Iraqi Girl," February 23, 2007, http://news.yahoo.com/s/afp/20070223/ts_alt_afp/usiraqjusticetrial_070223145608 (site discontinued).

31. Elsa McLaren, "US Troops 'Raped and Burned' Iraqi Girl, Court Hears," *Times Online*, August 7, 2006, http://www.timesonline.co.uk/tol/news/world/iraq/article602731.ece.

32. British Broadcasting Corporation News, "Rape Claim Splits Iraq Government," February 20, 2007, http://news.bbc.co.uk/1/hi/world/middle_east/6378821.stm.

33. Haifa Zangana, "We Have Not Been Liberated," *Guardian*, March 6, 2007, http://commentisfree .guardian.co.uk/haifa_zangana/2007/03/iraqi_womens_empowerment_under.html.

34. Ibid.

35. "Report of the International Committee of the Red Cross (ICRC) on the Treatment by the Coalition Forces of Prisoners of War and Other Protected Persons by the Geneva Conventions in Iraq During Arrest, Internment And Interrogation," February 2004, http://cryptome.org/icrc-report.htm.

36. "Could you tell us what happened?" Wolfowitz asked General Antonio Taguba. Someone else asked, "Is it abuse or torture?" At that point, Taguba recalled, "I described a naked detainee lying on the wet floor, handcuffed, with an interrogator shoving things up his rectum, and said, 'That's not abuse. That's torture.' There was quiet." In Seymour Hersh, "The General's Report," *New Yorker*, June 25, 2007.

37. Amnesty International, "Beyond Abu Ghraib: Detention and Torture in Iraq," March 6, 2006, http://web.amnesty.org/library/index/engmde140012006.

38. Michael Moss, "Country in Tatters Has a Legal System to Match," *International Herald Tribune*, December 18, 2006.

39. Jim Muir, "Iraqi Kurds 'Tortured Prisoners'," BBC News, July 3, 2007, http://news.bbc.co.uk/2/hi/middle_east/6266328.stm.

40. Among organizations involved in documenting the detention of Iraqi women are several independent women's and human rights groups operating inside and outside Iraq, such as Iraqi Women's Will, Occupation Watch, Iraqi Rabita (Iraqi League), Human Rights Voice of Freedom, and the Iraqi Committee for National Media and Culture, and international agencies and human rights and antiwar organizations (Amnesty International, the International Red Cross, the UN Assistance Mission in Iraq, and the BRussells Tribunal).

41. Jonathon Gatehouse, "U.S. Torture Scandal in Iraq," *Maclean's*, May 17, 2004, http://www.thecanadianencyclopedia.com/index.cfm?PgNm=TCE&Params=M1ARTM001260 4.

42. Andrew Buncombe and Justin Huggler, "The Torture Victim: Iraqi Tells How He Was Stripped, Beaten and Sexually Abused by US Military," *Independent*, May 6, 2004.

43. Often Iraqi collaborators help to promote such impressions. On April 18, 2004, Ministry of Interior Chief Ahmed Youssef issued a statement denying abuses of female detainees. He said, "We are Muslims. We know very well how to treat our female detainees."

44. Professor Ammash was the only female in the Iraq Command, the eighteen-member council that ran the Ba'ath Party. A mother of four, Ammash received her undergraduate degree at the University of Baghdad before traveling to the United States to study for her doctorate in microbiology at the University of Missouri, a degree she was awarded in 1983. She did extensive research on the effect of DU on Iraqi health and environment. Though described by the United States as "Mrs. Anthrax," she was released from the airport prison on December 2005. Nicknamed "Dr. Germ" by UN weapons inspectors, Rihab Rashid Taha, a microbiologist, was educated in England, earning a doctorate from the University of East Anglia where she studied plant disease. She was not on the US list of fifty-five most-wanted Iraqi officials, but the US still sought her capture. She was released on December 2005.

45. Laura Mansfield, "The Hooded Man from Abu Ghraib: The Rest of the Story," *Free Republic*, December 27, 2005, http://www.freerepublic.com/focus/f-news/1547528/ posts.

46. British Broadcasting Corporation, "Iraq Abuse Allegations Multiply," BBC News, May 10, 2004, http://news.bbc.co.uk/ 1/hi/world/middle_east/3698879.stm.

47. Agence France Presse, "Iraqi General Tells of Prison Torture Horror," December 12, 2005.

48. Seymour M. Hersh, "The General's Report," *New Yorker*, June 25, 2007, http://www.newyorker.com/reporting/2007/06/25/070625fa_fact_hersh.

49. United Nations Development Fund for Women (UNIFEM), February 23, 2005.

50. *Al-Taakhi*, December 6, 2006. (In Arabic.)

51. Abdul-Bassat Turki, the first Iraqi Minister of Human Rights, is the only Iraqi minister who resigned in protest against the human rights violations under occupation. Turki told the *Guardian* on April 20, 2004, that he had warned Bremer repeatedly of the abuses of prisoners in Abu Ghraib to no avail, and that he also phoned him to complain about the treatment of female detainees. "They had been denied medical treatment. They had no proper toilet. They had only been given one blanket, even though it was winter," Turki said.

IV. RESISTANCE

1. Support for the coalition forces based in Iraq is low, with 82 percent expressing a lack of confidence in them, and 69 percent thinking they have made the security situation worse. See British Broadcasting Corporation, "Iraq poll 2007," BBC News, March 19, 2007, http://news.bbc.co.uk/1/hi/world/middle_east/ 6451841.stm.

2. The UN General Assembly Resolution 33/24 of December 1978 affirms "the legitimacy of the struggle of peoples for independence, territorial integrity, national unity and liberation from colonial domination and foreign occupation by all available means, particularly armed struggle." http://www.un.org/documents/ga/res/33/ares33r24.pdf.

3. Brookings Institution, *Iraq Index: Tracking Variables of Reconstruction and Security in Post-Saddam Iraq*, July 30, 2007, http://www3.brookings.edu/fp/saban/iraq/index.pdf, 24.

4. David Kilcullen, "Twenty-Eight Articles: Fundamentals of Company-Level Counterinsurgency," *Iosphere*, Summer 2006, 29–35, http://www.au.af.mil/info-ops/ iosphere/iosphere _summer06 _kilcullen.pdf.

5. Jawad al-Khalisi, "The Gates Of Hell Are Open In Iraq," *Guardian*, April 2, 2005.

6. See Riverbend, *Baghdad Burning* (blog), http://riverbendblog.blogspot.com/2003_12_01 _riverbendblog_archive.html.

7. Phil Reeves, "Iraqi Rage Grows After Fallujah Massacre," *Independent*, May 4, 2003.

8. British Broadcasting Corporation, "What happened in Majar al-Kabir?" BBC News, June 25, 2003.

9. Nabil Y., "Iraqi Social Newsletter," *Alnawwab* 9 (November 2006). (In Arabic.)

10. Sabians or Mandaeans are followers of John the Baptist (called Yahya in both Mandaic and Arabic), who is recognized by the Christians and Muslims. They live mainly in Amara, southern Iraq and the Iranian province of Khuzestan. There used to be 50–60,000 Sabians in Iraq, but the figure has been reduced to a few thousand since the occupation.

11. Excerpts from speeches made by Hana Ibrahim of Iraqi Women's Will during her visit to Britain, December 6–11, 2005, to attend the peace conference organized by the Stop the War Coalition in London.

12. Ibid.

13. An e-mail received from Hana Ibrahim on March 28, 2006, 2:42 p.m.

14. See Knowledge for Iraq Women Society, http://almaarefa.org.

15. On April 23, 2006, a US patrol arrested an Iraqi woman with two "terrorists." She was accused of hiding explosives under her abaya. The Multi National Forces' statement about this incident was available at http://www.mnf-iraq.com/Releases/Apr/Arabic/060423d.htm, but the page has been discontinued.

16. British Broadcasting Corporation, "Iraq Says Women Killed Troops," BBC News, April 5, 2003, http://news.bbc.co.uk/1/hi/world/ middle_east/2917107.stm.

17. A woman sniper was arrested by joint US-Iraqi troops attacking Baquba, northeast of Baghdad, on June 25, 2007. See Aliraqnews.com, http://www.aliraqnews.com/modules/news/article.php ?storyid=27637. (In Arabic.)

18. Integrated Regional Information Networks, "Iraq: Killings Drive Women to Become Suicide Bombers," March 8, 2007, http://www.irinnews.org/Report.aspx?ReportId=70582.

19. Nicholas Blanford, "Iraqi Artists Depict Anger over Abu Ghraib," *Christian Science Monitor*, June 15, 2004.

20. E-mail from Zeina to the author, December 12, 2006.

21. The film *Iraq: The Women's Story* was shown on British Channel 4 on May 8, 2006. See http://www.channel4.com/news/dispatches/war_on_terror/the_womens_story.

22. Author's interview with Intisar, December 28, 2006.

23. Natasha Walter, "No One Knows What We Are Going Through," *Guardian*, May 8, 2006.

24. Hassan was one of five actors in *Caricature*, a forty-five-minute satire on al-Sharqiya TV that did not hesitate to make fun of police taking bribes and government officials whose main goal in life is lining their own pockets and leaving the country to protect their own safety. See Associated Press, "Fans Mourn Iraqi Comedian Gunned Down in Baghdad," *International Herald Tribune*, November 20, 2006, http://www.iht.com/articles/ap/2006/11/20/news/ ME_GEN_Iraq _Killed_Comedian.php.

25. Kasim Abid is a cameraman, director, and producer of Iraqi origin. He was educated in Iraq (Institute of Arts) and Russia (Moscow Film Institute, VGIK), and has lived in London since 1982. See "Kasim Abid," Arab Film Festival, http://www.arabfilmfestival.nl/directors/Kasim%20Abid.htm.

26. Integrated Regional Information Networks, "Singing 'the Devil's Music' Will Get You Killed," November 23, 2006.

27. Crisis Group, "What Can the U.S. Do in Iraq," *Middle East Report* 34 (December 22, 2004).

28. Dr. Mari Maeda, a researcher at the Defense Advanced Research Projects Agency (DARPA), says the government has spent $15 to $20 million a year over the past five years developing the mobile translator technology, because there aren't enough human translators to go around. Xeni Jardin, "Tech Solutions to Iraqi-U.S. Language Barrier," NPR, November 13, 2006, http://www.npr.org/templates/story/story.php?storyId=6480428.

29. Renae Merle, "First Ears, Then Hearts and Minds, Facing Shortage of Arabic Interpreters, Pentagon Seeks a Technological Solution," *Washington Post*, November 1, 2006.

30. Poet and art critic May Muzaffar was born in Baghdad and currently lives in Amman. She has published three volumes of poetry, many translations from Arabic into English, and several collections of short stories. "Snapshots" was received from her in June 2006. Translated from Arabic by Peter Philips.

31. Riverbend, "The Promise and the Threat," *Baghdad Burning* (blog), August 28, 2003, http://riverbendblog.blogspot.com/2003_08_01_riverbendblog_archive.html.

32. The Stop the War Coalition was formed on September 21, 2001, at a public meeting of over two thousand people in London. Its aim is to put an end to the "War on Terror" declared by the United States. It believes that "any war will simply add to the numbers of innocent dead, cause untold suffering, political and economic instability on a global scale, increase racism and result in attacks on civil liberties." See the Coalition's Web site: http://www.stopwar.org.uk.

33. Voices in the Wilderness was formed in 1996 to nonviolently challenge the economic warfare being waged by the United States against the people of Iraq. Voices continues its work today, acting to end the US occupation of Iraq. See the organization's Web site: http://vitw.org.

34. Iraq Occupation Focus, campaigning to end the occupation of Iraq, was formed in the spring of 2004 by a group of activists from across the antiwar movement who were spurred into action by the revelations of human rights abuses coming out of Iraq, the growing evidence of plunder by US corporations, and the appalling death toll inflicted by the occupying military forces. Iraq Occupation Focus, "About Iraq Occupation Focus," http://www.iraqoccupationfocus.org.uk/about.htm.

35. The World Tribunal Web site, http://www.worldtribunal.org, has been discontinued.

36. BRussells Tribunal, "Questioning the New Imperial World Order: The BRussells Tribunal," http://brusselstribunal.org.

37. Iraqi Democrats Against Occupation was formed by a group of progressive Iraqi activists involved since 1991 in the committee of Iraqi Democrats Against War and Sanctions. It continues a cam-

paign of solidarity with the Iraqi people in their struggle to end the illegal military occupation and to build a free, democratic, and united Iraq. See the organization's Web site: http://www.idao.org.

38. See the Web site for Solidarity for an Independent and Unified Iraq: http://solidarityiraq.blogspot.com.

Acknowledgments

This book, especially the historical part, is the result of my almost daily discussions with Mundher Al Adhami, who was, as always, generous with his time, support, and ideas. His tolerance and foresight made me see some of our contemporary political events differently.

Special thanks to my editor, Amy Scholder, who had to decipher her way through unfamiliar names, ancient places, and rapidly changing events, showing deep understanding and respect for the continuous struggle of Iraqi people.

Thanks to Sabah Zangana for his immense support, and to Orass Faruq for finding ways to send me the required books despite all risks involved.

Thanks to my friends: Nada Khouri, David Wilson, Kamil Mahdi, Scheherazade Qassim Hassan, Mohamed Kamil Aref, Wen-Chin Ouyang, Judy Cumberbatch, Peter Philips, and Sana Al Khayyat, for reading and suggesting changes and new references. Thanks to Safira Jamil Hafiz and Lahai al-Dami for sending me their books and rare texts on Iraqi women, and to Anisa Abdul Hadi (Um Laith) for telling me about the first schools in Iraq.

I am indebted to the late Professor Abdul Illah Ahmed, our prominent literary critic, who was, despite illness, willing to answer all of my questions about Iraqi fiction writers and the role of intellectuals under occupation.

About the Author

In 1958, when Haifa Zangana was just eight years old, Iraqis flooded the streets in celebration of their newfound, hard-won freedom from British colonial rule, which had begun in 1917. Zangana came of age in one of the most open societies in the Middle East—until it was shut down in the 1970s by the tyrannical, yet secular, Ba'ath Party. Joining in armed struggle against Saddam Hussein, Zangana was captured, imprisoned, and tortured as a young woman. She was released from Abu Ghraib after six months of detention, and has lived in exile ever since. Today, Haifa Zangana is an Iraqi political commentator, novelist, and former prisoner of Saddam Hussein's regime. She is a weekly columnist for *al-Quds* newspaper and a commentator for the *Guardian*, *Red Pepper*, and *al-Ahram Weekly*. She lives in London.

About Seven Stories Press

Seven Stories Press is an independent book publisher based in New York City, with distribution throughout the United States, Canada, England, and Australia. We publish works of the imagination by such writers as Nelson Algren, Russell Banks, Octavia E. Butler, Assia Djebar, Ariel Dorfman, Coco Fusco, Barry Gifford, Lee Stringer, and Kurt Vonnegut, to name a few, together with political titles by voices of conscience, including the Boston Women's Health Collective, Noam Chomsky, Angela Y. Davis, Human Rights Watch, Ralph Nader, Gary Null, Project Censored, Barbara Seaman, Gary Webb, and Howard Zinn, among many others. Seven Stories Press believes publishers have a special responsibility to defend free speech and human rights, and to celebrate the gifts of the human imagination, wherever we can.

For more information visit www.sevenstories.com.